LOW-COST
MARKETING RESEARCH

LOW-COST MARKETING RESEARCH

A Guide for Small Businesses

Keith Gorton
Hull College of Higher Education

and

Isobel Carr
College of the Bahamas

*Prepared under the auspices of the
Industrial Marketing Research Association*

JOHN WILEY & SONS

Chichester · New York · Brisbane · Toronto · Singapore

Library of Congress Cataloging in Publication Data:

Gorton, Keith.
  Low-cost marketing research.

  Bibliography: p.
  1. Marketing research.   2. Small business.
3. Marketing research—Great Britain.   4. Small business—Great Britain.
  I. Carr, Isobel.
  II. Industrial Marketing Research Association.
  III. Title.
  HF5415.2.G565 1983   658.8′3   82-17390

  ISBN 0-471-90077-X

British Library Cataloguing in Publication Data

Gorton, Keith
  Low cost market research.
  1. Marketing—Handbooks, manuals, etc.
  2. Small business—Great Britain
  I. Title   II. Carr, Isobel
  658.8   NF5415.12.8/

  ISBN 0-471-90077-X

Typeset by Pintail Studios Ltd, Ringwood, Hampshire.
Printed by Page Bros. (Norwich) Ltd.

Dedicated to Cathy

Contents

viii

Preface

This book was inspired by the Industrial Marketing Research Association (IMRA) at a time when the British economy is becoming increasingly dependent on the skill, inventiveness and success of small businesses. The brief for the book was clear: 'Make it possible on reading the book to give those organizations with severe cash restraints the confidence to embark upon a well-conceived and relevant marketing research project.'

The implications from the authors' point of view are clear; make the book short, simple and practical. Easier said than done!

In addition to the support from IMRA we are greatly indebted to the help and encouragement of our employers, Hull College of Higher Education. Judy Watling, in particular, has shown great patience and understanding when typing our various thoughts.

Thanks are also due to all those companies and trade associations who responded to our requests for up-to-date information on their activities.

KEITH GORTON
Hull

Chapter 1

Introduction and Scene-setting

Most texts on marketing research have been directed towards those students or industrialists who are likely to control large budgets to support marketing efforts. They are written with either a consumer marketing or an industrial marketing emphasis. The small-budget researchers in the industrial or the consumer sectors are generally overlooked. From this perspective alone one could be forgiven for believing that marketing research is only effective and desirable in situations where large amounts of time and money are available. We do not share this view, and hence this book, the objective of which is to provide the tools of marketing research to those with only small budgets at their disposal.

Decision-making in a rapidly changing world is dependent for a large part on the validity and reliability of the information supplied to the decision-maker. Marketing research does not make the decisions. There will always be a need for managers with judgment, intuition and sound commonsense. Marketing research, does, however, give the manager an unbiased view of the circumstances affecting his particular decision; in short, it leads to better, more professional decision-making.

This book is designed for those organizations who do undertake, or intend to undertake, research on a small budget. It will be of most interest to small companies and those large organizations who are critically reviewing the extent of their research budgets, hoping that they can get more for their money.

At the outset we must stress our commitment to research that attempts to embrace the highest ideals of professionalism and ethics. The research undertaken should, at all times, conform to the Code of Conduct issued by the Market Research Society and the Industrial Marketing Research Association, which is printed in full in Appendix 1.

Researchers are often tempted to forget the implications of the code. The temptation to use information provided in good faith by respondents for sales purposes is an insistent one that should, at all times, be resisted. Equally, there is no reference to 'industrial espionage' within these covers.

This book should be read in conjunction with the *Manual of Industrial Marketing Research*.[1] Many other references will be given, but the text should stand alone as a practical guide for the provision of meaningful marketing research. It is intended for small-budget researchers, whether they are involved in commercial, industrial, consumer or social research. Any company or organization wishing to

1

achieve a profitable and durable penetration of a market, be it an industrial, consumer or a social organization, must base its marketing strategy upon a thorough understanding of customer needs and wants, and be totally familiar with the buying process utilized by that customer and the factors that influence that customer in his or her choice. It is only through sound and thorough research that such an understanding can be attained.

Thus although there are many apparent differences between industrial, consumer and social marketing the principles are constant. It is in the application and the emphasis of these principles that the true differences emerge.

The following chapters are primarily concerned with the principles of good, sound research and are therefore relevant to any researchers, whatever market is being investigated. How those principles are applied may well differ, depending on the needs and requirements of the individual reader.

1.1 MARKETING RESEARCH

We are purposely not listing any standard, academic definition of marketing research. As Crosier[2] found when he researched definitions of marketing, it is difficult to find one that will be appropriate in all circumstances. We view marketing research in the small-business context as that activity that provides the decision-maker within the company with the best available information on which to base his decisions.

Marketing decisions are not the only ones a small-business manager has to make; he needs to plan his production, personnel and cash requirements. Information is needed to help him. The marketing research activity should be able to provide the information needed in all functional areas. The starting-point must always be: What information do the decision-makers need?

The main decision areas for which the marketing researcher may be required to provide the information input are, as McCarthy[3] points out:

(1) Product decisions.
(2) Promotion decisions.
(3) Pricing decisions.
(4) Place decisions.

A checklist of questions that a researcher may be required to answer has been included in Appendix 2. This, plus any questions of particular relevance to your own organization, should prove a useful *aide-mémoire* at the outset of a marketing research study. The reader is encouraged to take advantage of this appendix and not, as so often happens, assume that the appendices are for padding purposes only!

1.2 FOUR STEPS IN INFORMATION-PROVISION

The simplest of all models is the 'OPAR' model (Figure 1). OPAR stands for the

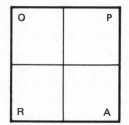

Figure 1.   The 'OPAR' model

four steps of the information provision process, i.e.

(1)   Objective;   O
(2)   Planning;   P
(3)   Action;   A
(4)   Review.   R

It is important that *all* the steps in the process are carefully considered. There is nothing more damaging to research than to jump straight in at the deep end by arranging a few interviews. The objective-setting and planning stages are sometimes considered a waste of time, and very few researchers take the time and trouble to review critically the work they have done. All too often the researcher is keen only to execute the work itself. 'Act in haste and repent at leisure' is never more true than when placed in a research context. We will now go through each of the steps in the information-provision process.

Objective

The first step is to decide what information is needed and why. Often the information is needed to solve your own problem, but on many occasions you will be required to understand another manager's problem. When this is the case, make sure that terms with which you are unfamiliar are carefully explained. Check that both parties' understanding of the problem is the same. Then probe, by asking why the information is needed and how the results will influence the decision-making. If the response to this probing is a series of comments such as 'It would be nice to know ...' or 'I've wanted to know for some time ...,' then kill the project. When you are working with only a small budget at your disposal, you cannot afford to be involved in aimless research. An objective, if it is to be effective, must meet the following basic criteria:

(1)   Is it commercially worthwhile?
(2)   Is it concrete and definite?
(3)   Is it achievable?

Commercially Worthwhile

The end-product of successful research should be increased profitability for the company, whether it be measured in monetary terms or in some other way. Research must come under the same close scrutiny as any other activity within the company. What are the cost implications of a research objective? A good example of a non-commercially worthwhile research objective was presented in the brief of a manufacturer of trailers who wanted to know the potential of his product. When probed on the specific segment(s) of interest, he replied 'All of them'. The researcher was directing his efforts to many different sectors, namely:

(1)   Domestic market;
(2)   Industrial market;
(3)   Agricultural market;
(4)   Armed Forces;
(5)   Nationalized industry;
(6)   Export.

The manufacturer placed the researcher in an unenviable position—he was being forced to research *all* sectors badly, because of the fixed nature of time and money available.

Definite and Concrete

The objectives must be precisely stated. When an objective is expressed in vague terms, there is very little likelihood that it will be achieved. Objectives that are quite commonplace are:

(1)   Find the market size for a product;
(2)   Find the companies operating in a certain field.

But the researcher needs to know the depth and degree of accuracy of the information required. The market size for a product can be presented as an order of magnitude—say, between £10–12 million per annum—or a precise measure—say, 69 units per annum. When finding out about companies operating in a certain field, does the sponsor require simply the name and address, or is more specific information called for? Without concrete and definite objectives, the work cannot be realistically measured.

Achievable

The above example of the trailer manufacturer's objective did not satisfy the third criterion for an effective objective either. It was simply not able to be done. Everyone seems to want information 'yesterday' and many research programmes reflect this haste. This is not to say that research cannot be effectively carried out quickly, but often bad, rushed research is in some ways worse than no research at all. Our advice is, if you do not have the time to do the research properly, then it is often better not to do it at all.

Planning

For each objective the researcher must think through the steps so that each piece of information required by the objective can be achieved. The planning phase should concern itself with answering the following checklist of questions:

Who will do the work?
When will the work be done?
Where will the work be done?
How is the work to be done?
How much will the work cost?

A timetable for the achievement of the steps should be drawn up with care being taken to ensure that the programme is sequential and well ordered. The schematic time-plan illustrated in Figure 2 shows a possible timing for a personal interview questionnaire survey.

Action

In order to plan a research programme effectively, careful consideration will have to be given to the steps and action that it will be necessary to take to achieve the objectives.

The following chapters will discuss in detail the elements of a marketing research programme and the steps generally taken by the marketing researcher to acquire the necessary information. Thus by an examination of these chapters the reader will be in a position to answer the questions: Who? When? Where? and How?

As in all research, the first step will be an investigation of the information already available on the subject of research. In Chapter 2 the possible sources of such information are examined. As pointed out earlier, often this may be all that is necessary to achieve the research objective. It is often surprising how many full-scale marketing research exercises are quite unnecessarily inaugurated simply because the researcher was not aware that the information already existed.

In further chapters we will examine how questionnaires are designed, how samples are taken and how interviewing can be effectively carried out; all of which are critical to the success of a research project.

Whether the reader decides to carry out the research himself or employ someone else to do it, (a question discussed in Chapter 5) an appreciation of the techniques involved will ensure the effectiveness of any research that may be undertaken.

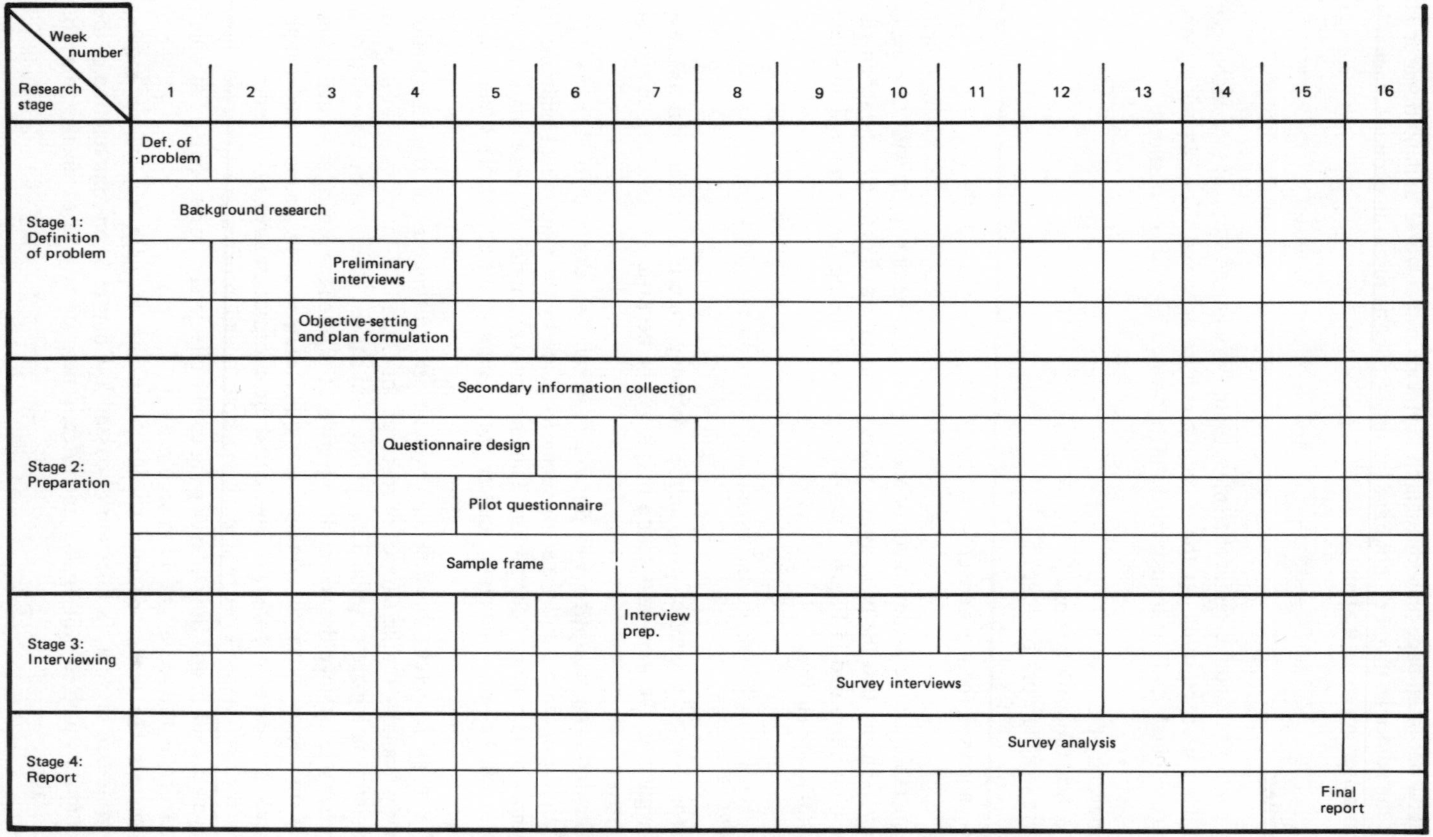

Figure 2. A schematic time-plan for a questionnaire survey

Review

The final, and often neglected, phase of the work is reviewing critically the exercise from start to finish. We do this not only to check that our objectives have been achieved but also to reinforce the elements of the learning we have experienced during the exercise. Many times an important source of information is lost because of not formally taking down the details whilst the memory is still fresh. It is self-defeating not to make a complete review, as in time the research programme reviews become the accumulated knowledge of years of practical research experience.

1.3   CONCLUSION

Good marketing research is best achieved by good habits. In particular the following model is recommended:

Objectives.
Planning.
Action.
Review.

1.4   CASE STUDIES

The following case studies identify the sort of problem areas that the small-business marketing researcher may face and give some indication of the steps to be undertaken in a research programme.

1.   The Case of the Restaurant's Rating

The Client

The client was a company operating hotels, restaurants and public houses. The particular concern was with one of their restaurants.

The Problem

The restaurant concerned had been acquired eighteen months previously. Since the time of the takeover business had gradually declined. The owner was worried that there had been an adverse reaction to the takeover and decided to investigate:

What kind of image the restaurant has;
How the image of the restaurant compares with that of competitors;
To what extent the restaurant is known;
What type of person is attracted to the restaurant.

The Survey

The survey consisted of 200 interviews in six different locations around the city. The sample covered both male and female, a broad spread of ages and socio-economic groups.

The Findings

The findings were as follows:

Respondents who had been to the restaurant were well satisfied with the services;
The image of the restaurant was quite favourable compared with that of competitors;
There was a low level of awareness of the existence of the restaurant in certain locations of the city;
The restaurant was frequented by middle-class people mainly from three of the locations covered on the sample and generally for what was termed as special occasions.

The Benefits

Prior to the research the restaurant-owner feared that the decline in business was due to an adverse image. After the survey he was able to ascertain that his major problem was that, although the restaurant had a favourable image, it was not one attended by people on a frequent basis, neither was it generally well known throughout the city. Having this knowledge, he was able to implement a promotional policy and decide on a policy strategy for the future of his business.

2. The Case of the New Product Decline

The Client

The client was a small importer of domestic and industrial equipment operating throughout the UK.

The Problem

The client had the opportunity of importing and selling under licence a piece of equipment new to the UK which the overseas manufacturers claimed had a wide industrial, public utility and domestic usage. The client would be involved in considerable initial costs and wanted to know if there was a market for the equipment before committing himself. A decision had to be made within two weeks.

The Survey

Given the shortage of time, interviews with potential buyers and users of the equipment were carried out by telephone. Seventy-five interviews were carried out using an open-ended discussion approach. Reactions to the product were obtained and contrasted with users' attitudes to the existing products, for which it was hoped that the new product would be an effective substitute.

The Findings

The survey showed that the market in the UK was much less extensive than that estimated by the manufacturer. It was possible to estimate:

That the type of model being offered was unsuitable for the UK market;
That existing competitors were operating at prices well below the price level required for the imported model;
That the technical back-up required to service the equipment was greater than the client envisaged;
The likely number of units the market might take.

The Benefits

The findings demonstrated to the client that what appeared to be an opportunity for increased profits would, in fact, probably be a costly failure.

3. The Case of the Hexagonal Nut

The Client

The client was a valve company manufacturing a valve with a hexagonal nut.

The Problem

A study showed that the unit would be 20% cheaper using a differently shaped nut. The problem was to find whether the user would be interested in the change.

The Survey

The survey consisted of a postal questionnaire survey to 500 industrial users throughout the UK. The sample included both customers and non-customers.

The Findings

The survey showed that users were indifferent as to the type of nut used, so that by using the cheaper nut the company would be more competitive in the market place.

The Benefits

The findings demonstrated to the client that there was increased market opportunity in manufacturing the cheaper nut without any derogatory effect on the valve's marketability.

4. The Case of the EEC (or not)

The Client

The client was a manufacturer of instant accommodation units operating from Hull/Humberside.

The Problem

Having found it increasingly difficult to penetrate the UK market the company wished, in view of its geographical position, to investigate the potential markets in the EEC. The problem was:

To identify the potential markets;
To identify potential distributors.

The Survey

A desk research survey was carried out. Information was gathered from various libraries, the British Overseas Trade Board and various export organizations.

The Findings

From the research it was possible to establish:
Market profiles of all the relevant countries.
A profile of competitors already in the market.
Information on potential distributors established in EEC countries.

The Benefits

The client was able to decide, on the basis of information provided,

Which of the potential markets to enter;
What was required of the company in order to penetrate the European market;
Which organizations could distribute his product.

5. The Case of the Ineffective Advertising

The Client

The client was a manufacturer of agricultural trailers.

The Problem

The client regularly advertised in various journals and wished to establish the effectiveness of his advertising.

The Survey

Personal interviews were carried out amongst 150 potential buyers and users. Recall and reactions to the advertisements of the company compared with those of competitors were assessed. It was also possible to find the type of journals read by the respondents.

The Findings

The findings showed that:

The respondents' recall of the advertisements of the company was low compared with that of competitors' advertising;
A large proportion of the respondents read magazines and journals not considered by the company.

The Benefits

The findings identified the magazines and journals where the company's advertis ing would be most effective and identified the type of advertisement the potentia buyer most easily recalled.

Chapter 2

Information Collection: Desk Research

To many, the image of marketing researchers is that of a body of people who spend their time armed with pens and questionnaire pads bombarding unsuspecting respondents with a profusion of questions which the latter often cannot answer, after which they write up a report containing remarkable evidence of previously unearthed facts.

In fact, nothing could be further from the truth. Like any effective research, before any expensive fieldwork is carried out marketing research begins at the desk, ploughing through the information which is already available. Hence any effective researcher must have a wide knowledge of the data in existence, its reliability and, most important, how it can be easily obtained.

Information sources can normally be divided into two main categories:

(1) Primary information; information which is to be collected for the first time by questionnaires, observations and other fieldwork methods.
(2) Secondary information; existing information which has previously been collected and reported by some individual or organization, and can be collated by desk research.

The importance of secondary information sources should not be underestimated. An effective secondary information system can, in many instances, save the need for potentially expensive fieldwork, or at least act as a solid information base from which those information gaps, which can only be filled by fieldwork, can be identified.

It is for this reason we have devoted this chapter to secondary information sources, as this is where the effective researcher will begin. The basic objective is simply to survey the potential sources of information in the UK and to give a guide as to where and how you can set about obtaining information required. The sources of information refer to the UK market only. Sources of information for overseas research will be discussed in Chapter 7.

2.1 INFORMATION NEEDS

Before any search for information begins it is necessary to decide what information is needed. Having thought clearly about the problem at hand, the next stage is

12

to draw up a list of the information required to solve the problem along with a list of potential sources of information.

The reader may find the market research checklist included in Appendix 2 useful in identifying the information needed to solve a particular marketing problem. In the following sections possible sources of information that may be useful to the reader are discussed.

2.2 INFORMATION COLLECTION: IN-COMPANY

In marketing research it is important that the researcher does not isolate himself, and assume that he is the only person within the company with any knowledge of the subject under research. If he does, he will find it self-defeating in the long run, because

(1) Others interested in the project often have a much greater vision and frequently have a wider experience base than the researcher;
(2) It is quite likely that much of the information is already held somewhere in the company.

There are many advantages in having an effective management information system within the company, ensuring that important information is communicated to the relevant parties, in the field of marketing research. Often quite valuable information is bypassed because of the lack of knowledge of its existence.

In most companies information is usually available in the particular department or section concerned with the following:

(1) Sales: an analysis of sales by product, area, etc.; customer profiles; competitive pricing and marketing activities.
(2) Purchasing: contacts with representatives from other companies; information and literature on products offered to the company; terms of sales, credit requirements of other companies.
(3) Accounts: status reports on customers supplied by the company.
(4) Archives/Records: records of previous work carried out in the area being researched.

Thus it is important in any research to ensure that full communication lines are developed with other company departments so that important information is not overlooked and that all relevant information is passed to the researcher. This point will be further examined in Chapter 5, where the question of who shall do the research is discussed.

2.3 INFORMATION COLLECTION: OUTSIDE THE COMPANY

When internal information sources have been exhausted there are many external sources the researcher can turn to to aid him in his research. These sources can be divided into public, commercial and educational.

(1) Public sources are frequently free of charge and can offer a great amount of help to the researcher. These are governmental statistical sources, public business libraries and the Department of Trade's Small Firms Division.

(2) Commercial services often charge a subscription fee. However, again, the advantage of using these sources is not to be underestimated because, if used effectively, the money is often well spent and can save a company much of the cost that would have been incurred if they had had to collect the information for themselves. The commercial sources surveyed in this chapter are the information services of the *Financial Times*, ASLIB, trade and research associations, chambers of commerce and banks (who often give a free advisory service to customers).

(3) Educational establishments are often overlooked as a potential source of information. More research is conducted in universities, polytechnics and colleges than any other sector of business life. Learn to tap this source and many potential benefits will accrue.

2.4 PUBLIC SOURCES OF INFORMATION

Governmental Statistical Services

In the UK we have one of the best government statistical support services in the world. Although its major objectives are to serve the needs of the government, the information it compiles is readily available to the business community.

The first point about government statistics is that each department publishes its own statistics and publications. However, information can be derived from more general publications such as

(1) *Trade and Industry.*
(2) *Business Monitors* (giving quarterly sales information for over 5000 product lines).
(3) *Monthly Digest of Statistics.*
(4) *Social Trends.*

A very helpful little booklet called *Profit from Facts* is published by the Central Statistical Office, giving many illustrations of how government statistics may be used. The following checklist illustrating how government statistics may be relevant to your business appears in the booklet. It is thought worth repeating here. The appropriate publications are given in brackets.

Checklist

Which of the following are relevant to your business? Government statistics can help you:

MARKETING ☐ To assess market share trends in a large number of product fields; to watch size and growth of existing and potential markets (*Business Monitors*)

☐ To count the number of potential customers; their size and characteristics; regional pattern—to compare with your own customers in order to spot weaknesses in marketing strategy:

Farmers (*Agricultural Census*)

Manufacturing firms (*Census of Production*)

Construction industry (*Housing and Construction Statistics*)

Retail shops and service establishments (*Census of Distribution*)

Hotels and restaurants (*Catering Trades Enquiry*)

Educational establishments (*Statistics of Education*)

Persons and families (*Census of Population: Social Surveys; Inland Revenue Statistics*)

☐ To see how people spend their money (*Family Expenditure Survey; National Food Survey; National Income Blue Book*)

☐ To check on distribution channels (*Census of Distribution*)

☐ To monitor price changes—retail prices (*Department of Employment Gazette*); wholesale prices (*Trade and Industry*); agricultural prices (Ministry of Agriculture, Fisheries and Food Press Notices)

☐ To use retail sales and stock movements to assist short-term sales forecasting (*Trade and Industry*)

☐ To assess the possibility of meeting foreign competition in home markets; to calculate your share of UK exports (*Overseas Trade Statistics of the UK*; Customs and Excise Bill of Entry Service)

☐ To estimate world markets (Statistics and Market Intelligence Library; Department of Industry)

☐ To fix quotas for area salesmen (Regional Statistics)

BUYING ☐ To be aware of the sales trends of materials and goods supplied to you (*Business Monitors*; Customs and Excise Bill of Entry Service)

☐ To trace the price movements of materials (*Trade and Industry*—the Department of Industry also constructs some price index numbers to meet specialized requirements)

PERSONNEL ☐ To watch trends by industry and by region in unemployment, vacancies, earnings, overtime, wage

rates, hours of work, industrial disputes; and compare
with your own situation (*Department of Employment
Gazette; British Labour Statistics Yearbook*)

MANAGEMENT ☐ To compare your firm's results with those of other
EFFICIENCY firms
AND FINANCE ☐ Operating ratios—net output per head as a percentage
of sales, wages per £ of total sales, etc. (*Census of
Production*); stock/turnover ratio, gross margin, turn-
over employee, etc. (*Census of Distribution*)

☐ Labour costs (*Department of Employment Gazette*)

☐ Company finance—aggregated balance sheets;
appropriation accounts; sources and uses of funds;
income, interest and dividend payments as percentage
of assets; analyses by listed/unlisted companies and
industry analysis; liquid assets of companies (*Business
Monitor M3: Company Finance; Financial Statistics*)

CONTRACTS ☐ Where an escalation clause is needed, to consult the
Departments of Trade, Industry and Employment
about the most suitable price indices for materials and
labour costs

☐ Property Services Agency produce indices for use with
the National Economic Development Office's price
adjustment formulae (Monthly Bulletins of Construction Indices)

COMPANY ☐ To assess the current replacement cost of your fixed
ACCOUNTS assets and stocks (Price Index Numbers for Current
Cost Accounting)

Central Statistical Office

(1) The Central Statistical Office (CSO) publishes a very helpful annual document called *Government Statistics—A Brief Guide to Sources*. This details the
publications of the CSO giving telephone numbers and contact points. The
booklet can be obtained by writing to:

Press and Information Sources
Central Statistical Office
Great George Street
LONDON SW1P 3AQ.

(2) Two very good contact points if you have any difficulty obtaining a publication you require are:

Department of Trade
Statistics and Marketing Intelligence Library
1 Victoria Street
LONDON SW1H 0ET (telephone: 01-215-5444/5)

and

Business Statistics Office
Cardiff Road
Newport
Gwent NP7 1XG (telephone: Newport 56111, Ext. 2973).
(3) Most government publications are stocked at your local central library.

Cost

All published information is available free of charge from public libraries. If you have to go further and seek special tabulation from the department a charge may be made.

National Economic Development Office

The National Economic Development Office publishes many reports on particular sectors of industry which may be of interest to the researcher. NEDO publications are listed in a free booklet entitled *NEDO in Print*. This can be obtained from:

NEDO Books
1 Steel House
11 Tothill Street
London SW1 9LU.

2.5 BUSINESS LIBRARIES

A business library is very useful as a quick reference service for inquiries of any commercial nature. They are generally located at the local central library and exist in most towns. The services they are able to provide vary from town to town, but access to a library providing a full range of services should not be a problem, as these can be found in many locations throughout the country. The largest is the City Business Library, London, but other business libraries can be found in Teeside, Hull, Cardiff, Glasgow, Dundee, Sheffield, Manchester, Birmingham, Liverpool, Leeds, Aberdeen, Belfast and Edinburgh. The following services are provided.

Abstracting Services

McCarthys, a newspaper-cutting service of corporate and industrial news from the national and the provincial press.
Extel, a financial abstracting service, providing detailed financial information on approximately 1000 British quoted companies.
Dun & Bradstreet, a credit-reporting service which is an excellent aid in producing fact sheets on both public and private concerns.

Company Reports

A monthly cumulation of live companies registered with Companies House, updates daily;
Reports and accounts of all major companies together with cutting files on local business.

Trade Names

The Patent Office index to World Trade Marks provides details of thousands of trade names both in the UK and abroad.

Statistics

All UK government statistical series together with major EEC, OEDC, UN statistics and annual abstracts of other foreign statistics organizations.

Market Reports

Mintel Publications Limited, a service providing reports on consumer goods markets and services.

Directories

A wide range of directories providing detailed information on both British and foreign companies; telephone and telex directories for the whole of the UK, Europe and the majority of other countries.

Contact

The local central library of the town in which the business library you wish to consult is located. Use of the enquiry service can be made by telephone or telex, letter or personal visit.

Cost

No charge is made for the service available.

2.6 DEPARTMENT OF INDUSTRY: SMALL FIRMS DIVISION

The Small Firms Service was set up by the Department of Industry in 1976. Its major objective is to provide information and counselling services to help owners and managers of small businesses. The Division operates through a nationwide network of small firm centres which provide the following services.

Dial-an-Answer Service

This excellent 24-hour service which is provided throughout the network of small firm centres is extremely useful as a contact point. If you have a problem that is hard to solve, or if you are in need of information that you cannot find, these services will put you in contact with experts.

Information and Counselling Service

The Small Firms Counselling Service (SFCS) again operates through the network of small-firm centres. The SFCS gives you the opportunity to talk over any marketing or marketing research problems you may have with the Small Firms Counsellor, an experienced businessman in the field of management, and if a specialist is required then the SFCS can put you in touch with specialist consultants and advisors.

Cost

There is no charge for the Dial-an-Answer service or for any straightforward enquiry. The first session with any counsellor is free, although should further consultations be necessary then moderate charges may be made.

Contact

Contact can be made by telephone, telex, letter or personal visit to the centre nearest to you. A list of all centres is given below.

Small-firm Centres

To call the Centres on Freefone dial 100 and ask the operator for the Freefone number.

Northern Region

22 Newgate Shopping Centre, Newcastle-upon-Tyne NE1 5RH
Tel: Newcastle 25353, Freefone 529
Telex: 537429 SFICNR G

North-West Region

Peter House, Oxford Street, Manchester M1 5AN
Tel: 061-832 5282, Freefone 6005
Telex: 667952 SFICNW G

Sub-office for Liverpool

1 Old Hall Street, Liverpool L3 9HJ
Tel: 051-236 5756, Freefone 6005

Yorkshire and Humberside Region

1 Park Row, City Square, Leeds LS1 5NR
Tel: 0532 445151, Freefone 5361
Telex: 557687 SFICYH G

East Midlands Region

48–50 Maid Marian Way, Nottingham NG1 6GF
Tel: Nottingham 49791, Freefone 4062
Telex: 557687 SFICYH F

West Midlands Region

53 Stephenson Street, Birmingham B2 4DH
Tel: 021-643 3344, Freefone 372
Telex: 337919 SFICWM G

Eastern Region

35 Wellington Street, Luton LU1 2SB
Tel: Luton 29215, Freefone 372
Telex: 826115 SFICER G

London and South-Eastern Region

65 Buckingham Palace Road, London SW1W 0QX
Tel: 01-828 2384, Freefone 2079
Telex: 917920 SFICSW G

South-West Region

Colston Centre, Colston Avenue, Bristol BS1 4UB
Tel: Bristol 294546, Freefone 9910
Telex: 449650 SFICSW G

Scotland

57 Bothwell Street, Glasgow, G2 6TU
Tel: 041-248 6014, Freefone 846
Telex: 779334 SFICFC G

Wales

16 St David's House, Wood Street, Cardiff CF1 1ER
Tel: Cardiff 396116, Freefone 1208
Telex: 497515 SFICWA G

2.7 COMMERCIAL SOURCES OF INFORMATION

ASLIB (Association of Special Libraries Information Bureau)

The ASLIB organization works for the achievement of two basic objectives. First, its aim is to improve the effectiveness with which the world's resources of knowledge and information are used by industry, commerce, scholarship and research. To this end it works as a national documentation centre in the field of information transfer and as such offers the following services to industry.

(1) It provides consultancy services for those who require help in designing and operating information units of any kind.
(2) It maintains a library devoted to information science and documentation.
(3) It runs training courses, seminars and conferences covering most aspects of information handling.

Companies endeavouring to maximize the efficiency of the use of in-house information may find these services very helpful.

Second, the aim of ASLIB is to provide direct help to any member-organization in finding and obtaining specific information on any subject of current interest. The ASLIB information department provides four major services which small firms in need of help in this area may find very helpful:

(1) Referral and inquiry service: this service is designed to answer requests for information on any subject and in any depth by carrying out searches or referring the enquirer to sources of information;
(2) Bibliographical checking service: this is designed to help an inquirer who knows that a certain document contains useful information but cannot specify the document reference precisely. ASLIB will help to certify the existence of the document and provide an accurate reference;
(3) The interlending service: ASLIB, with its series of location indexes, is able to arrange for the inquirer to obtain access to documents which have proved inaccessible through other channels;
(4) English translation of foreign materials: ASLIB maintains the Commonwealth Index of Unpublished Translations. This contains over a quarter of a million entries and it is advised that this index be consulted before commissioning a translation. If the translation exists then it can easily be obtained: even if it does not exist, ASLIB are able to recommend a translation from its Registrar of Specialist Translators.

Contact

The ASLIB headquarters are located at 3 Belgrave Square, London SW1 8PL (telephone: 01-235 5050).

Cost

The services are free to all members. The subscription for members varies depending upon the size of the organization, but once the subscription has been paid a member is able to use as many services as desired and as often as required with no extra charge.

2.8 BANKS

Banks should not be omitted as an important source of marketing information. All major banks now offer an advisory service to industrialists on a wide range of problems outside the areas of finance. Although they do not claim to be experts in marketing they have, through wide experience of firms seeking their advice, a working knowledge of the macro-environmental factors and how they influence the industrial businessman.

Contact

Your local bank manager will inform you of the services available at your own bank.

Cost

The services are usually free of charge to existing customers. If you do seek the services of another bank offering an advisory service then a charge will be made to non-customers.

2.9 FINANCIAL TIMES

The *Financial Times*, as well as being an important source of information in itself, also has an information service which is widely recognized in the effective contribution it has made to industry. Established in 1971, it offers a broadly based impartial business intelligence service covering all aspects of national and international industry and commerce. (The international aspects of this service will be dealt with in Chapter 7.)

The base for the service is the extensive *Financial Times* Library and a staff of qualified and expert researchers. Its major services are the following:

Provision of Company Information

The service has close links with FINTEL, a company jointly owned by the

Financial Times and Extel to develop electronic information services for the business community. Through the MIRAC Service the *Financial Times* provides microfilm copies of annual reports published by over 3000 public UK companies.

Provision of Marketing Information

Drawing from a wide range of sources the information service is able to answer queries on a variety of marketing-related subjects, for example:

Brand shares;
Advertising expenditure;
Company logo usages;
Trade mark registrations;
Production, import, export, sales figures by industry;
Profiles of companies in a particular industry;
Purchase and usage patterns for a given product in a given market.

Provision of Financial Information

The *Financial Times* is considered the most authoritative source for much of the current and historical information published in the UK. Examples of financial information offered are the following:

Financial statistics;
Foreign exchange rates;
Money market movements;
Commodity prices;
Stock and share information;
Property prices;
Economic and business indicators.

To increase the scope and flexibility of the statistical information offered, the *Financial Times* has a terminal for accessing on-line databases such as the Central Statistical Office, Eurocharts and International Financial Statistics.

Special Projects

This service undertakes special tasks and will carry out extensive research into a given area. The aid given falls into three main categories:

(a) A special investigation into a given area;
(b) A monitoring service of a given area, thus providing up-to-date information on any particular field of interest;
(c) Aid in the setting up of a new library information system and in developing and improving existing facilities. (In this area the Information Service works closely with ASLIB.)

Contact

Financial Times Business Information Limited, Bracken House, 10 Cannon Street, London EC4 4BY.
Telephone: 01-248 8000, Ext. 7087 or 334
Telex: 8811506

Cost

Subscriptions can be on a six-monthly or annual basis. The minimum annual subscription is £150 (excluding VAT) and is deposited with the information service when the subscription is taken out.

Each enquiry is costed according to the time taken, based on an hourly rate of £20 and debited against that deposit. The special report service is charged on a fee basis, the fee being dependent on the research time and expenses involved.

2.10 COMPANIES HOUSE (REGISTER OF BUSINESS NAMES)

The Register of Business Names based in Cardiff and London holds company reports on all limited companies in the UK since the formation of the companies concerned. These records are no longer available for public inspection but can be obtained through agents. For example:

Extel,
ICC Legal Services,
OYEZ Services.

The only service they now give to the public is the identification of the address of a company if the full name and correct title of the company is known.

Contact

Companies Registration, Office, Crown Way, Maindy, Cardiff.
Telephone: 0222 388588
or
London Search Room, Companies House, 65–71 City Road, London EC1.

2.11 RESEARCH AND TRADE ASSOCIATIONS

There are numerous trade and research associations in the UK today which may be a potential source of reference to the industrial market researcher. However, it must be remembered that their responsibilities are confined to individual subject areas and, unlike public services or libraries, their first responsibility has to be to their members, and understandably, many are wary of making their knowledge available to non-members.

As such, services to non-members tend to be regarded as a matter of public relations and goodwill. Thus the association will probably answer enquiries providing that they do not involve the association to the detriment of members' interests.

In the course of the research for this chapter a letter was sent to 130 associations to ascertain the services offered to members and non-members, and the price and qualifications for membership. The response was varied, as over 50% of the addressees did not even reply. Of those that did, the services ranged over the complete spectrum, from nothing to associations making every effort to assist in any way possible.

Trade Associations

It is the larger and more sophisticated trade associations which are most likely to be in a position to help the market researcher with his enquiries. Services that may be offered by such an association are:

(1) The provision of the opportunity for members to exchange information on commercial and technical matters and channels of communication to external organizations;
(2) A monthly newsletter giving new statistical and general information to members;
(3) Library facilities;
(4) The sponsorship of trade shows;
(5) Activities of a technical nature in respect of the products of members and the application of those products.

Trade associations can also be of help to manufacturers involved in export. The services offered in this direction will be discussed in Chapter 7.

Research Associations

Research associations may be independent but are often linked to a particular trade association. In the past they have largely been limited to carrying out pure and applied research in the furtherance of industrial development, but there are significant changes of direction in progress. One such example is the Rubber and Plastics Research Association, whose services are:

(1) An annual guide to commercial information sources pertinent to the rubber and plastics industry;

(2) An economic and information unit offering a wide range of commercial services and supplementary publications.

The above is only one example: such services are now being offered by the more progressive research associations.

Contact

CBD Publications Limited[4] publishes an excellent directory of British Associations. It provides a single quick reference point for locating and identifying associations, societies, institutions and organizations relevant to the field of enquiry. Once the relevant associations have been identified it would be advisable to contact them individually to ascertain requirements for membership and the services that they are able to offer.

Cost

The membership fees of trade and research associations vary enormously, but it may be that a small company will find it necessary to pay around £300 per annum to join a reputable and progressive association.

2.12 CHAMBERS OF COMMERCE

The information and library services of the local chamber of commerce are usually restricted to members only. Across the country the quality of their information services varies considerably.

The largest chamber in the UK is the London Chamber of Commerce. This offers extensive services, has an excellent commercial library and is widely acclaimed as an important source of aid for business and commerce. Other notable chambers of commerce with information services are those of Birmingham, Leicester and Liverpool. However, the smaller chambers have much to offer the local manufacturer simply because of the genuine interest by chambers in their local members.

The major advantage of being a member of a chamber is the superb network of contacts it has both in the UK and abroad. Thus if your local chamber is not in a position to help you it will most certainly find the person or organization which can.

The chambers of commerce can also be a source of aid to the UK exporter, and the services offered in this direction will be discussed in Chapter 7.

Contact

The telephone number and address of your local chamber can be found in the telephone directory. Your local business library will be able to help you identify the relevant person to contact regarding your enquiry.

Cost

The membership fees of the chambers vary between £20 to £50 per annum for a small company.

2.13 EDUCATIONAL ESTABLISHMENTS: COLLEGES AND UNIVERSITIES

General Services

A great number of very useful market research projects are carried out by colleges, polytechnics and universities, and basically these can take the following forms:

(1) Projects carried out as an integral part of a student's course. These are variously described as thesis, projects, assignments, etc. but, whatever the name they may be a source of useful information for the local industrial firm. Unfortunately very few institutions have catalogued these projects. Thus it is a matter of enquiring at your local institution to find if the research of your interest has been carried out;

(2) Consultancy assignments by lecturing staff. Most members of management studies departments in colleges and universities welcome the opportunity to become involved in research assignments especially if

(a) The area of study is of particular interest to the lecturer and it would be possible to publish the results of the research either in college or as an external paper;

(b) Your company provides the college with students.

Contact

The director or principal of your local institution will give you the names of the course tutors in marketing and management studies. These tutors will be able to advise you on the work that has been carried out by students and also discuss the possibility of any consultancy assignments.

Cost

Copies of student projects will normally be made available free of charge, requiring only the permission of the tutor and the student involved.

The cost of consultancy assignments is variable and normally negotiable with the member of staff concerned. However, most college-based consultants will be prepared to work for quite moderate charges if the criteria (a) and (b) specified above are met.

University Business Libraries

The universities of Coventry and Warwick and the Manchester Business School all have excellent business library facilities and provide information services to non-university personnel. For example, the Warwick University library is fully staffed with qualified librarians and experts to guide your desk research activity and can offer the following services:

Enquiry Service

An enquiry can be made for anything from a specified figure to a dossier of tables, articles, reports and other documentation covering such areas as:

Production and sales figures;
Products and industries;
Market size and shares;
Imports and exports;
Economic conditions;
Company financial data prices;
Advertising expenditure.

Research Analysis

If you require detailed analyses or a written desk research report, special arrangements can be made.

Monitoring Service

If you need a particular figure on a regular basis, e.g. the price index for your particular industry, but you do not subscribe to the source, the service will 'flag' the source in their system and periodically send you a copy of the relevant table when it is issued.

Newsletter

Subscribers receive a monthly newsletter containing reviews of major industry services, new statistics sources and articles from a wide range of business-related journals and periodicals.

Library Services

Bibliographic and literature searches can be undertaken using the wide range of abstracting and indexing sources available.

Contact

Enquiry can be made by telephone, telex, letter or personal visit to The Warwick Statistical Service, University of Warwick Library, Coventry CV4 7AL. Telephone the Statistics Librarian (0203 62530) or the Economics Librarian (0203 24011, Telex 31406).

Cost

An annual subscription of £200 is made. This includes the enquiry service, library services, the newsletter and personal visits with staff assistance. Enquiry time used in excess of 20 hours during the 12-month period will be charged an excess of £10 per hour or parts thereof.

If it is unlikely that you will need to use the service on a regular basis it is available to non-subscribers at £10 per hour (£1 minimum). The fees for all other services will be negotiated on an individual basis depending on the requirements involved.

2.14 CONCLUSION

Obviously not all the services of every source discussed in this chapter will be of relevance to any particular problem you may be researching. Even so, it is useful to have knowledge of the data sources available and how to contact them. Figure 3 is a summary chart of the organizations surveyed. It may be useful to ascertain your local contact in each of the services mentioned, enabling you at a glance to know how to contact any organization which may aid you in the search for the information required.

2.15 FURTHER REFERENCES

It is not practicable to detail all sources of information here. However, in the experience of the authors, the following references have proved very useful for research purposes.

Indexes

Research Index: An annual guide, by industrial categories, to articles and news items of financial interest from over a hundred periodicals and the national press. Published by Business Surveys Limited, PO Box 21, Dorking, Surrey.
Business Periodicals Index: A subject guide to all articles in English-language periodicals.
Published by H. W. Wilson Company Limited (USA).
British Technology Index: A subject guide to all articles in UK technical journals. Published by The Library Association.

30

SOURCE	CONTACT	ADDRESS	TELEPHONE NUMBER
In-company			
Sales			
Accounts			
Purchasing			
Records			
Public			
Government statistics			
Business library			
Small-Firm Centre			
Miscellaneous			

Commercial			
Bank			
Financial Times			
Companies House			
ASLIB			
Associations			
Chamber of commerce			
Trade association			
Research association			
Educational			
University			
Polytechnic			
College			

Figure 3.   Contact sheet: potential sources of local information

Company Directories

Kompass: Volume 1, A detailed directory of suppliers of products and services; Volume 2, A detailed directory of company information.
Published by IPC Business Press Limited.
Kelly's Directory of Manufacturers and Merchants.
Published by IPC Business Press Limited.
Times 1000: A review of the top 1000 leading companies in the UK and overseas.
Published by Times Books.

Marketing Information

Tupper and Wills, *Sources of UK Marketing Information.*
(Marketing Research Society).
Published by Ernest Benn Limited.
MGN Marketing Manual: A useful source of summary data relating to consumer marketing.
Published by Mirror Group Newspapers Limited.
BRAD (British Rate and Data): Index to publications containing detailed media information.
Published by BRAD, 76 Oxford Street, London W1M.
Mintel Market Reports: Monthly published market reports on consumer goods markets and services.
Published by Mintel Publications Limited, 20 Buckingham Street, London WC2 6EE.
The Market Research Society, *Organisations Providing Market Research Services in Great Britain:* A useful directory of market research agencies and organizations providing market research services in the UK. Available from The Market Research Society, 15 Belgrave Square, London SW1X 8PF.

2.16   CASE STUDY

The following is an example of a Research through Secondary Information Collection.

6.   A Preliminary Investigation into the UK Market for Machine Tools

A machine tool manufacturer was in the process of deciding whether or not to build a new plant in the north of England. Tools manufactured at this plant were intended for the UK market.

Problem

An analysis of the UK market was required:

(1)   To draw up a profile of the current UK market;
(2)   To identify market opportunities;
(3)   To assess the market potential;
(4)   To obtain a profile of developments in the market.

Survey

The preliminary survey was based on secondary information collection in order to assess the feasibility of carrying a full-scale primary research survey. Information was collected from the following sources:

(1)   Trade Associations; from the Machine Tool Trade Association information was collected on:
    (a)   Competitive manufacturers in the UK;
    (b)   Production statistics of the machine tool industry;
    (c)   Names and addresses of contacts;
    (d)   Through correspondence with the contacts the researcher was able to obtain a profile of developments in the UK machine tool industry.
(2)   From the Statistical and Marketing Intelligence Library information on the following was obtained:
    (a)   Import and export statistics by product;
    (b)   *Business Monitor* statistics giving import and export statistics of UK manufacturers.
(3)   City Business Library (London); from information available at the City Business Library profiles of the competitive manufacturers were drawn up from:
    (a)   Extel cards;
    (b)   *Kompass*;
    (c)   Company reports.
(4)   Press; current financial and investment information and general market information was obtained from:
    (a)   *Financial Times*;
    (b)   Major national newspapers;
    (c)   Trade journals.
(5)   Published Reports; from the BOTB directory of published market research reports a report was located on the UK machine tool market giving valuable information on the user industries and potential developments in the various industries.

Findings

It was found that the market was in a slow upward movement out of a recession and that users of machine tools were at present planning future investments in new plant equipment.

34

Benefits

From the preliminary research the company was able to identify market opportunities in particular areas. As a result the company was able to carry out a full-scale research project into the particular areas of interest only, thus making effective use of time and research resources.

Chapter 3

Information Collection: Field Research

Regrettably, not all the information we need is available from secondary sources: on some occasions field research methods must be used. However, more care should be taken, as field research requires a greater degree of technical competence from the researcher as well as more resources both in time and money.

This chapter is divided into four main sections:

3.1 Observation techniques
3.2 Direct questioning via individual and group interviews
3.3 Postal and telephone surveys
3.4 Other methods, including the use of panels, folder tests, hall tests and test markets.

All methods should be considered against the research objectives to determine those which offer the most likely success rate against projected costs.

3.1 OBSERVATION TECHNIQUES

In this research method, widely used in anthropology and other areas of scientific study, the interviewer (observer) gathers the information by observation rather than by questioning respondents. The method has achieved a high degree of sophistication in consumer research, where advanced technology has provided the researcher with cameras and other recording devices such as the psycho-galvanometer (which measures the perspiratory rate of the respondent). This text contents itself with simply using the natural faculties of sight, smell and hearing.

Examples of Using Observation Techniques

(a) In many companies it is difficult to forecast the demand for products because the demand is distorted due to the stockholding of the intermediaries, i.e. merchants, stockholders, etc. The sales force, in some instances, can check the stock levels by simply observing the stocks as part of their routine. The simple form shown in Figure 4 was designed by a company producing steel panel radiators. The representative was asked to complete the form on a monthly basis. Happily the merchants co-operated, being satisfied that this service was in their interests.

35

Company Address:		Tel. No.		
Date	Brand in stock	Type & approx. volume		Comments
		Single	Double	
5.1.80	Myson Stelrad	2 000 20 000	5 000 10 000	

Figure 4.   Stock level inventory form

(b) All companies have to decide whether or not they will rent space at a trades fair. Organizers of such events can be guaranteed to provide very optimistic assessments of their benefit to the potential participants. It is therefore useful to visit an exhibition to observe its nature, assess the number of visitors, explore the traffic flow and determine the best-sited and attended stands.

(c) The way a product is used is not always as intended. Observing the product in operation could expose several myths associated with its use. Following products on their journey from producer to final user can give a useful insight into important areas such as packaging, the necessity for assembly instructions and possible new applications for the product.

(d) Accompanying a representative on his calls is a useful information-provider. The way the company's case is presented and the obstacles the sales force meet are brought into focus.

Seeing at first hand how the various promotional items are actually used can offer guides to a more effective promotion policy.

How to Use Observation Techniques Effectively

Delens[5] defines observation techniques as 'those whereby the investigator is placed in a position from which he can observe and note the actions and behaviour of respondents'. This definition has two implications for the researcher:

(1)   The activity should be observable;
(2)   The observer should have the facility to note the observations either simultaneously with the action or immediately after.

The following procedure is suggested to assist in ensuring that the observations are successful ones.

Pre-observation Phase

(1)   Decide quite clearly what is to be observed and the use to which the results of the work are to be put.

(2) Anticipate the problems of the observer. Will he be able to see/hear? How close must he get to the activity to have a reasonable chance of interpretation?

(3) Determine the best ways to record the results of the observation (written notes, checklists, tape recorder).

(4) Plan the time, date and circumstances of the observation.

(5) Decide on the level at which the observation is structured. In a completely unstructured situation no restriction is placed on the observer, whereas in the completely structured situation he only records those activities outlined on his checklist, ignoring the rest. In practice, a sensible balance is best, giving sound guidelines coupled with the encouragement to note anything else of interest.

Observation Phase

There should be no deviation from the plans and observation must be accurate. To avoid committing too much to memory, the observation period should be interspersed with reasonable breaks for recording those items which cannot be recorded simultaneously with the activity. Be aware of the observer's influence on the respondent, and beware of observing artificial situations.

Observations can be a cost-effective method of research but is totally useless if the observer allows personal bias or lack of objectivity to influence him.

3.2 DIRECT QUESTIONING (PERSONAL INTERVIEWS)

In consumer marketing research great emphasis is placed on the use of face-to-face interviewing; often this is the only way by which the mass consumer can be reached. The industrial situation is different; generally, industrial markets are dominated by a handful of customers, and the situation of 80% of the turnover being consumed by 20% of contacts is quite usual.

The small-budget researcher will rarely be involved in large numbers of interviews, and thus great care must be taken when choosing the sample to be investigated. Because of the relative importance of some customers and the intricacies and details of the questions that require answers, the face-to-face interview becomes necessary. The major advantages of the method are:

(1) Personal interviews have a better chance of acceptable returns, with a low respondent-refusal rate.

(2) The sample is less distorted, since it is not restricted by availability of telephone or the erratic response rate associated with postal enquiries.

(3) Observation techniques can be employed concurrently with the interview.

(4) The interview can be managed more effectively. A *rapport* can be developed between the interviewer and the respondent which can break down the natural suspicion that surrounds an interview.

(5) A much wider range of questions can be covered.

Interviews may be directed to individuals or groups. They also vary in length, content and the demands made on the interviewer. Some are highly structured, where a questionnaire has to be strictly adhered to; others are unstructured and in-depth. The less structured the work the greater the skill required by the interviewer.

Depth Interviews

The interviewer does not have a specific set of pre-specified questions that must be asked; instead he is guided by his brief, a checklist and his good sense. The interviewer is free to create questions and probe those responses that appear relevant. There is only one rule; he must not try to affect the content of the answers given by the respondent. There are normally two classifications of depth interviews:

(1) Non-directive
(2) Focused.

The essential difference between (1) and (2) is the amount of guidance the interviewer gives the respondent. In the non-directive interview the interviewer function is to

(1) Encourage the respondent to talk about a given topic with a minimum of direct questioning;
(2) Refrain from directing the course of the conversation along any specified lines;
(3) Probe with statements such as
'Tell me more'
'That's interesting'
'Why do you say that?'

the basic idea being that the respondent leads the interview. In contrast, the focused interview concentrates on a pre-selected checklist or prompts. However, the choice of questions and the timing of these questions is left to the interviewer's discretion. In a focused depth interview to learn more about purchasing decisions the interviewer might be instructed to cover areas such as finance, influence of customers, quality reliability, views on being entertained by representatives, value of exhibitions, etc. Within each of these areas the interviewer would be instructed to probe until he is certain that he has covered the underlying attitudes associated with that area.

Depth interviews are expensive, and normally a maximum of two can be completed in an interviewer day. At consultancy rates of around £150 per day, plus expenses, interviews can cost as much as £100 each.

In order to provide an accurate record of the interview a tape recorder can be used. However, if the interviewer decided to do this he must bear in mind that this can lead to the respondent being more cautious, self-conscious and tense. In particular, the inarticulate respondent can be very embarrassed by the sight of a tape recorder.

Group Interviewing

Group interviewing methods are seldom used by the small businessman. The main problems appear to be the difficulties in assembling the group and finding a sufficiently experienced person to lead them. However, he may find group interviewing techniques useful within his own company to organize, for example, a brainstorming session, or perhaps within his own trade at a club or association where potential respondents regularly meet.

Using this technique a number of carefully selected respondents are brought together and invited to discuss whatever topic is under review. A questionnaire may be provided but more usually the discussions are free-ranging. The spontaneity and stimulation of the group situation motivates a high number of creative responses and so is particularly useful to generate new product ideas, to determine attitudes and buying influences or to pilot studies testing vocabulary and buying decisions. Creative devices such as brainstorming rely heavily on group interaction.

Group interviews can be conducted with respondents who share the same interest, such as buying, or with groups having more diverse interests. In any event, the number of persons involved should never be less than four. The interviewer's role is crucial but more limited than in other situations. He normally introduces the topic and tries to ensure that the group does not deviate from it. Beyond that, he relies primarily on group interaction to produce the insights.

Generally, more detailed and accurate information can be derived from a group than from the individuals when each is interviewed separately. The interaction with others expands and refines the opinions of the individuals and a snowballing effect occurs when the comments of one trigger off ideas and feelings in the others. Interest in the topic is more easily stimulated in group situations and respondents often feel more secure, allowing themselves to relax and become more fully involved than in other types of interview.

3.3   POSTAL/TELEPHONE SURVEYS

Postal Surveys

The postal survey does not necessarily have to use the facilities of a post office but can be taken as any survey where the respondent is not contacted either visually or verbally. Thus the postal enquiry would include questionnaires that are placed in house magazines or other publications, those directed through the in-tray system in companies and that very useful basis of getting research information—the guarantee card. In the *Manual of Industrial Marketing Research* a postal questionnaire is regarded as a structured series of questions in written form sent to potential respondents which may, if necessary, be answered anonymously. This definition does not therefore include any general enquiry such as a letter, which might elicit information which does not make use of a formal series of questions.

Advantages of the Postal Questionnaire

(1) Most of the supporters of postal questionnaires point to the fact that postal enquiries are cheaper. This is generally because they base the cost calculations on the number of questionnaires despatched, not on the number of completed questionnaires returned, which would render them more expensive. Nevertheless if no incentives are sent, a questionnaire sent by post can be of reasonable cost.

(2) A more positive advantage is the width of distribution that can be achieved by the postal method. Respondents in outlying areas can be contacted as easily as those in the larger conurbations.

(3) Speed is often cited as being one of the key advantages of the postal method. This is legitimate, since if a respondent intends to reply he normally does so sooner rather than later. There will be stragglers, and it is not unusual for a questionnaire to be returned six months after the expected returning date, but, in general, a questionnaire is answered virtually immediately on receipt by the respondent.

(4) In industrial situations it is often very difficult for a respondent to find the time when he is behind his desk. This is particularly true in engineering markets, where site problems mean that traditional office hours are not observed. In this instance the postal method may prove advantageous.

(5) The postal questionnaire obviously eliminates interviewer bias. The key problem of telephone and face-to-face interviews is therefore overcome. The respondent can remain anonymous. This is a mixed blessing, since even though a respondent might sign that his position is one of seniority, the questionniare could have easily been completed by an assistant. In a recent survey further investigation showed that 18% of respondents held positions different from those given on the questionnaire.

Disadvantages of the Post Questionnaire

(1) There is a greater non-response problem with the postal questionnaire than with any other method. The number of respondents depends primarily on the interest that survey generates, either because of the nature of the questionnaire or perhaps because of the gift or other incentive that is made to the potential respondent. In some instances appallingly low response rates have been given, and any result generated in these circumstances must be highly suspect.

(2) A serious problem when dealing with postal questionnaires through traditional channels is the problem of obtaining a representative mailing list.

The problem is exacerbated in industrial markets, as job titles tend to differ substantially from company to company. In a small organization the managing director may be the key decision-maker of the products which are to be purchased; in larger organizations this could be the sole responsibility of a buyer.

(3)   The length of the questionnaire is obviously a restricting factor with this sort of enquiry. In the authors' experience it has been found that questionnaires are more likely to be filled in if the questions can be accommodated on, at maximum, two sheets of paper. This could be the most severely restricting limitation for any survey.

(4)   The counter to the advantages of anonymity are, of course, the increased likelihood of ambiguity, because the questions themselves cannot be enlarged upon by the interviewer. This disadvantage can be overcome by a thoughtful and well-organized pilot survey.

Postal Response Rates

Response rates vary considerably from as little as 2% to as much as 95% in the case of some guarantee cards. But what are those ingredients that make a postal enquiry successful? In order to achieve an effective response rate the following factors should be considered by the researcher.

(1)   The mailing list should have time spent on it; in fact, it is helpful to ring up a small sample of the companies on the mailing list to check the address of the company and whether the expected respondent still works at that company.

(2)   It is important that the envelope and the letter are addressed to a specific person. This ensures in most organizations that the questionnaire has a chance of being answered by an appropriate respondent. Where it is impossible to find the names of suitable respondents it is a widely accepted policy that the chief executive or the managing director should be the designated addressee, since it is most likely that, if necessary, they will pass on the questionnaire for response to someone more appropriate in the organization.

(3)   Make sure that the questions you are asking are of real interest. A well-presented questionnaire coupled with a really interesting topic does get surprisingly good responses. Perhaps this is the most crucial way to guarantee a successful postal questionnaire.

(4)   The covering letter and the questionnaire should be professionally printed and presented.

(5)   The questionnaire should not be more than two pages in length.

(6)   A reminder sent a fortnight after the initial questionnaire will normally bring about a 50% increased response rate; i.e. if the response to the initial questionnaire was 50% then, on completion of a first reminder, there will be a 75% response.

(7)   The use of incentives is beneficial to the response rate. A wide variety of incentives can be used, varying from all respondents taking part in some sort

of lottery for a variety of prizes to each respondent being guaranteed a gift of anything up to about £5 in value. But beware; no matter how attractive the gift, no matter how well-presented the questionnaire, no matter how detailed the research on potential respondents, if the study is a dull and uninteresting one, respondents will not materialize.

Telephone Surveys

Increasingly, the telephone method of enquiry is being used in the UK. Its increased popularity recently has stemmed from a number of successful surveys completed over the telephone. Indeed, there are very few market research exercises which do not have some element of telephone enquiry in them. The telephone is an excellent medium for being able to test a questionnaire.

Undoubtedly, there have been very exaggerated claims for this method of enquiry, and the reality of trying to reach respondents on the telephone can be very frustrating and unproductive. The most important ingredient in the telephone enquiry is the interviewer. People make mistakes by expecting the good-face-to-face interviewer to be a good telephone interviewer. One only has to think of how surprising the reality can be after you have made an impression of someone on the telephone to realize that we all have a telephone personality which may not be reflected in our physical personality. Therefore it is important that the interviewer is clearly briefed and thoroughly practised in the art.

There are many advantages put forward for the telephone enquiry:

(1) Cheapness: by cutting down the travelling time it is argued that far more of the interviewer's time is spent interviewing, and this means that the interviews themselves are cheaper.

(2) Speed in interviewing: claims have been made that good interviewers can complete as many as ten interviews in an hour. As a norm this would be quite remarkable; normally one would expect a maximum of five interviews per hour. However, an interview day of thirty to forty interviews cannot be scorned, particularly if some sequential analysis method is in operation (see Chapter 4).

(3) A wide geographical spread can be covered inexpensively. Telephone costs do vary with the distance from the respondent, and it is worth remembering that costs of calls vary at different times of the day. If possible, it is therefore better to use the telephone as an interviewing medium in the afternoon rather than the morning.

(4) The interviewer is able to take copious notes without affecting the respondent.

(5) The respondent is able to study information which may be of a confidential nature or look at a reference in his own office: this would be difficult for him to do if an interviewer was present. He might be quite prepared to look up things himself and pass information on, but may not be prepared to take the risk that an interviewer could see the source from which his information comes.

(6)   In comparison with the interviews conducted by post the telephone is extremely flexible, giving the interviewer the opportunity to explain in detail the nature and scope of the various questions.

The limiting features of the telephone enquiry are:

(1)   The interview length is generally more restricted than in the case of personal interviews, although this can be partly overcome by an effective interviewer. The authors have been involved with telephone interviews which lasted in excess of thirty minutes.
(2)   It is possible to use semi-structured questionnaires which would be totally inappropriate in the postal survey method.
(3)   The lack of eye contact with the respondent does increase the difficulty of the interview.
(4)   There is a sad shortage of good telephone interviewers!

Do's and Dont's

The *Manual of Industrial Marketing Research*[1] gives the following do's and dont's:

DO get the name of the appropriate respondent at once from the switchboard operator or, if put through to the wrong person, get it from him.

DO stress confidentiality and the IMRA/MRS code of conduct if challenged.

DO keep up the tempo and avoid pauses.

DO ensure that you make it possible for a call-back to be made to clarify any points or to elicit more details should they be required at a later stage. Such call-backs can also be used as an interviewer quality control.

DON'T give any details about the survey until you talk to your respondent.

DON'T allow secretaries to put you off. Be persistent and ask to speak to the respondent personally.

DON'T be frightened of the telephone or rebuffed by a series of unfortunate interviews.

3.4   OTHER METHODS

Panels

The panel method requires that the same group of informants be used on a regular basis over a period of time. The panel, normally recruited by personal interview, should be a representative cross-section of potential purchasers/influencers. The major advantage is that they allow research to be completed on a continuous basis and the results thereby obtained are directly comparable with previous ones.

Panel members can be contacted by telephone, post or face-to-face. Additionally, they may be asked to complete a diary of their activities. Panel members are normally paid or receive gifts for their services.

The advantages of this method are:

(1) The provision of trends and directly comparable data.
(2) The establishment of specific case histories.
(3) The creation of a source of marketing intelligence.

The disadvantages are:

(1) The difficulties in obtaining a panel which is not simply a collection of 'tame' contacts and of keeping the wastage on the panel down to a minimum.
(2) The expense involved in the recruitment phase, in panel visits and the rewards or incentives normally required.

One particular example of the panel method is the Delphi technique.

Delphi Technique

This eliminates committee activity by gaining a consensus through a series of postal questionnaires. A panel of experts is carefully selected and is asked to estimate either the year an expected phenomenon is likely to occur or to make an estimate of the value of a phenomenon. For example,

(1) In which year do you envisage that the majority of new vehicles sold will be driven by means other than petrol?
  or
(2) What do you predict will be the sales of domestic solar heating systems in five years' time?

The response estimates given by the panel are likely to spread over a wide range. A follow-up questionnaire is fed back to the respondents with a summary of the distribution of the respondents, stating the median response and the range of the responses.

The respondents are then asked to consider their previous answers and revise them as they see fit. If the answer is outside the range the particular respondent is asked to state his reason for thinking that the answer should vary so much from the majority.

Typically those without strong opinions will move towards the median. Those who feel that they have good arguments to support their opinion tend to retain their original estimate. At the end of the second round the responses are again distributed with a concise summary of the arguments put forward, and estimates are again called for. By this anonymous debate by questionnaire the Delphi method draws on the benefit of group work whilst avoiding the social compromise which normally occurs in face-to-face situations. Individual views can be argued, abandoned or sustained behind the mask of anonymity without loss of face and without being over-affected by personality, reputation or seniority of others. The rounds continue until a compromise is reached.

The greatest drawback to this method is the selection of the panel. Members need to have the seniority and the overall control to make effective judgements on the future.

Folder Test

Often the consumer does not see the product before he purchases it. Instead he makes his choice from leaflets, brochures or other printed matter. To test the acceptability of these methods a folder showing various alternative presentations can be shown to the respondent. The method lends itself very easily to sequential sampling methods (see Chapter 4).

Hall Tests

A hall can be hired to display alternative product designs. If the product is eventually used on a large scale then the hall test can be efficient and cheap. Most city centres have suitable halls available at reasonable cost. However, this method is only really suitable for industrial consumable and consumer products.

Alternatively, in the case of professional buyers, an hotel room could be selected near an exhibition centre to take advantage of those buyers attracted to the exhibition.

Test Markets

A test market situation, normally associated with the introduction of a new product, is one where a small area is used to indicate the likely national reaction. It is rarely used by small businessmen but the concept of a small market trial could be useful. For example, if the company is considering importing a product manufactured overseas a test market may be useful in alerting management to unsuspected problems and opportunities associated with the product.

3.5 INCENTIVES FOR RESPONDENTS

There is little doubt that providing respondents with gifts or cash does encourage a higher response rate. Response rates for postal questionnaires can be significantly improved by the offering of incentives. In some types of research an incentive is almost obligatory, for example:

(1) In group discussions some incentive is needed.
(2) Interviewing specialist professions such as plumbers, insurance brokers, builders merchants, etc.

(3) Interviews which require more than one visit, e.g. in testing a new valve the valve would have to be provided free of charge.

There is a clear distinction to be made between small-budget research and cheap research. All involved in market research, whether as respondents, companies or marketing research agencies, have a vested interest in maintaining high standards and respondent co-operation. Incentives help by retaining respondent interest in market research generally and ensuring that the company involved in the research thinks more carefully about the research design and does not discourage respondents.

If you do offer incentives make sure you offer the respondent the opportunity to decline. Some local authority employees have very strict rules imposed on their acceptance of gifts. Make sure you do not embarrass or compromise them.

Incentive Possibilities: Some Examples

Postal Questionnaires

We have found that gifts of up to £2 in value have significantly affected response rates. Care should be taken in selection of the incentive, bearing in mind the following points:

(1) The nature of the respondent;
(2) The ease of distribution of product;
(3) Flexible source of supply.

Pens seem universally acceptable and fortunately can be readily obtained. Catalogues of potential incentives can be obtained from sales promotion consultants. For the addresses contact:

(1) British Advertisers Gift Distributors Association, 33 Claremont Park, London NW3; telephone 01-346 4735.
(2) British Premium Merchandise Association, 46 Downs View Road, Maidstone, Kent; telephone 0622-55092.

Group Discussions

For a one-hour group discussion a £3–£5 food voucher plus mileage expenses is considered a reasonable incentive. Of course, if the product being discussed is of value in its own right it is possible that each contributor will be satisfied with the gift of the product itself.

Intellectual Respondents

The professions, academic and quasi-academic respondents are often motivated by having access to the final conclusions drawn by the researcher. Architects and consulting engineers are very eager to keep abreast of any innovation in their areas of specialism and often ask for a copy of the report, even when it is not offered!

Cost Checklist

Postal Survey Cost Build-up

Printing questionnaires
Envelopes
Covering letter
Postage (including reply-paid facility for respondents)
Incentive
Mailing incentives
Analysis and presentation
Researcher time

Telephone Survey Cost Build-up

Interviewer fee
Telephone charge
Questionnaire
Analysis and presentation
Researcher time

Face-to-Face Interview Cost Build-up

Interviewer fee
Interviewer expenses (mileage, etc.)
Questionnaire printing
Prompt-card printing
Incentive
Analysis and presentation
Researcher time

Group Discussion Cost Build-up

Recruiting group—interviewer fee
Recruiting group—interviewer expenses
Hire of room
Incentives
Consultant (group leader) fee
Consultant (group leader) expenses
Cost of tapes
Analysis and presentation
Researcher time

Observation Methods

Interviewer observer fee
Interviewer/observer expenses
Analysis and presentation
Researcher time

Of course, cost in each element will vary, but care should be taken that each element is budgeted for before the job takes place.

3.6 CONCLUSION

In this chapter we have outlined a series of primary research methods and indicated the potential advantages and disadvantages of their application. Care should always be taken in ensuring that the most realistic method to suit the time scale and the financial constraints is adopted.

Chapter 4

Sampling Methods

The notion of sampling is as old as the study of statistics itself. It was realized very early that to obtain a representative view of a group of people it was not necessary to interview them all; the problem is determining how many to interview to ensure that the views expressed do represent the group as a whole.

This chapter will discuss briefly the implications of taking samples and will describe several methods, with a step-by-step analysis of how the work might be used.

The sample size is often a compromise between the accuracy required and the amount of money available for the study. In general, the small businessman is constrained mainly by cost. It is therefore useful for him to have a rule of thumb measure as to how accurate the study really is. (Those readers who require a more statistical approach are directed to a series of texts in the Bibliography at the end of the book.)

Kurt Finsterbusch[6] makes a strong claim for the benefits of mini-surveys (between 20 and 80 interviews). We share the view that much of great value can be derived through low-cost, low-sample research. This is unlike the view of social scientists, who tend to be preoccupied with large-scale, expensive methods. Such research would probably be beyond the resources of the small businessman, unless perhaps he becomes involved in multi-client studies. (See Chapter 5 for a discussion of multi-client studies.)

There are two major types of sampling procedures:

(1) Probability or random sampling;
(2) Non-probability or quota sampling.

4.1 RANDOM SAMPLING

In this method each member of the population from which a sample is to be taken has an equal chance of being selected. You may feel that this is a simple sampling method but it is not. Random does not mean haphazard. For instance, asking your secretary to pick twenty names in no particular order from a telephone directory does not produce a random sample. Even though she may follow your instructions implicitly, the respondent selection will be influenced by the bias which is placed by her on the sample selection. Her eye may well be drawn to familiar names or short names. The best way is to use random number tables (see Appendix 3).

Method

Assume that you have a list of 1000 addressees and that from this list you wish to interview 100 people, i.e. 1 in every 10. Then take the random number tables and place them alongside the list of 1000 addresses.

As you wish to interview 1 in 10, then decide that all random numbers between 00 and 09 will be interviewed and that all random numbers between 10 and 99 will not be interviewed.

For example, in Appendix 3 the first number on the random number table is 03; thus the first addressee on the list will be interviewed. The second number is 47. As this is between 10 and 99 the second addressee on the list will not be interviewed. The third number is 43, so again the third addressee on the list will not be interviewed.

This process should be continued until the required sample is obtained.

Advantages/Disadvantages of Random Sampling

The major advantage of random sampling is that all statistical work such as significance testing assumes that the samples are random. The degree of sampling error can be statistically calculated, and comparability between samples taken at various times can be objectively assessed. It does, however, suffer from the following severe disadvantages:

(1) It assumes that an up-to-date list is available from which to select the sample. Anyone who has ever tried to compile such a list will tell you that this is virtually impossible. By the time any list is published several changes of names and addresses are bound to have taken place.
(2) By determining precisely who should and should not be interviewed the survey costs are made more expensive.
(3) It is more time-consuming than other methods.

The Errors that Occur in Samples

Even in the most perfect random sample the results extracted from the survey will contain a certain amount of error. It is possible, however, to calculate an estimate of the likely error that will occur in a random sample. The following examples explain the methodology.

Example

Assume that your survey is a simple question to which respondents answer either Yes or No. Then let

P = percentage saying Yes
Q = percentage saying No
N = size of sample you have taken.

Then you can be 95% confident that your results will be within the limits

$$\pm 2 \sqrt{\frac{P \times Q}{N}}$$

of accuracy. If 50% of respondents state Yes and 50% state No in a survey of 100 people, then

$P = 50$
$Q = 50$
$N = 100$

$$\text{Error} = \pm\, 2 \times \sqrt{\left(\frac{P \times Q}{N}\right)} = \pm\, 2 \times \sqrt{\left(\frac{50 \times 50}{100}\right)}$$
$$= \pm\, 2 \times \sqrt{25}$$

Error $= \pm 10\%$. Therefore you can be 95% confident that your results are accurate within $\pm 10\%$, i.e. between 40% and 60%.

Estimation of the Sample Size

Given that the researcher knows the percentage error acceptable to his survey, then by substitution it is possible to use the above equation to determine the optimum sample size, as can be seen in the following example.

Example

Assume that an acceptable error is $\pm 20\%$ for the results of the survey. Then the sample size can be determined by:

$$\text{Error} = 2 \times \sqrt{\left(\frac{P \times Q}{N}\right)}$$

$$N = 2 \times \frac{P \times Q}{(\text{error})^2}$$

Assuming a 50% Yes, 50% No possible response, then in our example

$$N = 4 \times \frac{P \times Q}{(\text{error})^2} = \frac{4 \times 50 \times 50}{20 \times 20}$$

$$= 25$$

Understanding the Sampling Equation

There are three very important features to be taken into account when using the equation

$$\text{Error} = \pm 2 \times \sqrt{\left(\frac{P \times Q}{N}\right)}$$

(1) As the sample size increases the error decreases: thus the survey becomes more accurate. But

(2) The error decreases proportionally to $\sqrt{(1/N)}$. Therefore an error decrease of $\frac{1}{2}$ requires the sample increasing by 4, an error decrease of $\frac{1}{3}$ requires a sample increase of 9! And so on.

(3) The equation does not take into account at any time the size of the population being tested. Thus error arising from a sample of 200 is the same regardless of the population being 10 000 or 10 million!

Non-sampling Errors

However, errors still remain which are due to non-sampling error, namely:

(1) Badly designed questions;
(2) Poorly presented questions;
(3) Respondent error;
(4) Analytical error;
(5) Presentation error.

The total of all these possibilities can be quite substantial. Thus in reality the non-sampling error can be greater than the sampling error.

4.2 QUOTA SAMPLING

In quota sampling the sample is selected at the discretion of the interviewer, who is given strict guidelines as to the number and nature of the respondent. An example of quota sampling might be as shown in Figure 5. The quota is selected to reflect the nature of the overall population being researched. In Figure 5, for

		Company size (fitters)				
		1	2–10	11–25	25+	
	North	3	10	10	2	25
Area	Midlands	3	10	10	2	25
	South	6	20	20	4	50
		12	40	40	8	100

Figure 5. Sampling a quota of heating engineers

example, we would expect 3% of the heating engineers' businesses to be one-man operations in the north of England.

Advantages/Disadvantages of Quota Sampling

The quota sample method is, in practice, most frequently used because of its speed, flexibility and cost advantage over the random sample. But the analysis of the sampling error is then, at best, an educated guess, and caution should be taken with any subsequent analysis. It is vitally important that the interviewer be correctly trained when quota sampling is used, or unacceptable bias may creep into the results.

4.3 OTHER METHODS

Cluster Sampling

Cluster sampling alleviates the problem of geographical dispersal in interviewing by concentrating surveys in selected clusters, e.g. particular counties, towns, sales areas or local authority boroughs.

Random sampling can be applied to this method if the clusters and the units within those clusters are selected in a predetermined way, for example, by drawing up a sampling frame of potential clusters and selecting the clusters to be sampled by using the random number tables discussed earlier. If this is done then it would be possible to also estimate the potential error in the sample (see page 51).

If cluster sampling is used but the clusters are chosen at the discretion of the interviewer then they will equally be as cost-effective, although, as in quota sampling, the analysis of the sampling error will only be an educated guess.

Sequential Analysis

In conventional techniques of market research described earlier it is necessary to pre-select a number of respondents, complete field research and then attempt a full analysis of data obtained. Sequential analysis is concerned with simple, cumulative analysis of results as they are obtained, and it enables field research to be terminated when sufficient evidence has been collected to provide definite answers to issues under investigation.

Sequential analysis techniques are particularly suited to problems which may be regarded as a 'dichotomy' (i.e. Yes or No, A or B).

Respondents are asked in turn to state a preference (e.g. Yes or No, A or B). The preferences are then plotted sequentially on a pre-designed chart which has marked boundaries to correspond with the 'stopping conditions'. When a sample path of the preferences stated reaches one of the boundaries, then it will be deemed that enough evidence has been collected to provide a definite answer and the investigation will be terminated at that point.

The major advantage of the method is that it is quick, simple and cost-effective.

However, it is only suitable for very simplistic questions and relies on a definite response. For the purpose of analysis, 'don't know' and 'no preference' responses are ignored. Occasionally it may be that these replies are sufficiently numerous to nullify the speed of the technique in obtaining results.

4.4 CONCLUSION

Sample selection should always be taken with great care, with the emphasis on commonsense rather than elegant statistical theory which is rarely understood. In this chapter we have discussed the two major sampling methods, i.e. random and quota sampling, and have briefly introduced other simple sampling methods. Always be aware of the problem of bias in your results by giving the sample selection phase of your work the thought and attention it deserves.

Chapter 5

Who is Responsible?

This chapter is concerned with the important question of who should do the work. In the small-business/budget situation there is a clear tendency for the company to attempt to complete the whole of the marketing research exercise itself. This could prove self-defeating, as concentration of one's own valuable time in only one area of marketing means that some other area is neglected.

Throughout this book it has been assumed that the reader wishes to understand what is going on so that he will be in a better position to utilize his own resources. However, reading this book alone will not create an effective researcher. Outside help will be needed to some extent, and so this chapter examines the following points:

5.1 Utilizing the Whole Company;
5.2 Utilizing the Outside Consultant;
5.3 Multi-client Studies.

5.1 UTILIZING THE WHOLE COMPANY

The discussion of the role of marketing research has so far mainly concentrated on research as consisting of individual projects. In chapter 2 we discussed the importance of seeking research information within the company before carrying out further stages of a research project. Research can also be conducted on a continuing basis as part of a marketing information system.

This system, vital in an increasingly changing and competitive environment, is again only successful when all functional areas and associated personnel play their part in the provision of information. The simple expedient of involving more than the marketing function in the information provision process has two benefits for the company:

(1) It focuses the attention of all personnel on the importance of the market-place, thus leading to a greater awareness and interest in the ultimate consumer;
(2) By spreading the responsibility it can uncover talents, energies and interests that would normally be overlooked.

All members of the company should be encouraged to note any market pointers they perceive. This may lead to duplication but the principle of too much rather than too little certainly applies.

To motivate non-marketing personnel it is helpful for the chief executive to take a lively interest in the information collection process. The type of information required and the use to which it will be put must be clearly spelled out and advice on recording information provided. Consider a small company with the structure as in Figure 6. Each area has a provision of information due to the peculiar nature of the department and the specialist nature of the management team. An example of specialist sources of information might be as shown in Figure 7. By the simple expedient of creating a forum where various topics and articles of interest can be recorded the company soon builds a useful picture of the environment.

Obviously, the planning of any *ad hoc* work is enhanced by interaction with

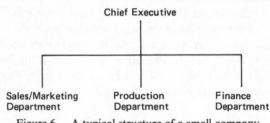

Figure 6.   A typical structure of a small company

POSITION	INFORMATION SOURCES
Chief Executive	Institute of Directors Bank manager Other local chief executives Trade associations
Production Manager	Institute of Industrial Managers Outside suppliers Stock control Engineers/trade press
Finance Manager	Credit agencies Accountant Bank manager Institute of Accountants Financial press Outside suppliers
Personnel	Manpower Services Commission Institute of Personnel Management Training board
Marketing	Sales force Institute of Marketing Trade shows Exhibitions Industrial Marketing Research Association

Figure 7.   An example of specialist sources of information

others' experience. The precise definition of the problem under review is better understood if it has to be explained to others. The 'devil's advocate' approach to proposals and expenditure ensures that only worthwhile exercises are undertaken. The method by which co-operation is achieved is a matter of style and circumstances; some companies have formed fairly clearly defined information committees, whereas others have allowed the more informal nature of day-to-day contact in the small-business environment to suffice.

Cost of own Company Personnel (1979 prices quoted throughout)

Researchers often forget that their own time and money should be costed against any project. Where costings are made they are often unrealistic. For the purpose of an example of how to cost one's own time we will assume the researcher is paid £5000 per annum. A car, pension and other fringe benefits would make his total cost around £10 000.

Assume that he works effectively about 5 days per week for 45 weeks. (52 total less 5 holidays less 2 for training/illness, etc.) Then the daily cost is

$$\frac{£10\,000}{45 \times 5} = £45 \text{ per day}$$

Assume overheads of around £5 per day and we are left with a rule-of-thumb cost for a researcher of around £50 per day.

Whilst £50 per day is less than half a normal consultancy rate it is much higher than the basic fee of £20–£30 per day for some interviewers who can be hired on a daily basis.

Of course, this analysis may be totally false. The company may have a young member of staff who will benefit from the experience of interviewing and other field work. The cost of this staff member may be closer to the bought-in cost of interviewing.

The Sales Force

To the company carrying out research on a low budget, using salesmen to carry out interviewing seems a highly convenient solution. However, the benefits of using salesmen for interviewing are questionable. Aubrey Wilson, in *The Assessment of Industrial Markets*,[7] discussed the use of salesmen in market research at length, concluding that it is highly undesirable. In the large company this assertation has much to commend it, but in the small company or for researchers operating on small budgets the sales personnel offer a possible basis for field work that might otherwise not be available.

It is important to understand the reasons why using a salesman could be a disadvantage. The very nature of the stereotype salesman, that of the aggressive, enthusiastic, persuasive and highly subjective order-seeker, projects an individual whose skills are the antithesis of those required by the objective researcher. His business is to sell, and time not selling can be costly to the company and himself personally if he is paid by commission. Thus in the course of a research exercise the salesman might be tempted to revert to selling from researching to take advantage of an opportunity that presents itself. However, the mobile nature of the salesman does allow interviews to be completed on a very marginal cost basis. Further, it helps reduce the feeling of isolation from the company that sales personnel often experience. On a small budget the use of the sales force will make many projects feasible.

The major responsibility of the researcher, apart from the obvious one of creating an atmosphere in the company where this sort of co-operation can exist, is to ensure that the sales force are fully trained in the techniques and skills of market research. The training programme should be seen as an extension of, or a replacement to, the usual sales meetings; the training board should be consulted, as it is possible that the training programme could be eligible for grants. If the company feels ill equipped to carry out the training programme, the business studies department of the local college will probably be prepared to design a course specifically to meet the company's needs. The very act of investing time in the development of other skills for the salesman will be perceived as a very mature approach from the company, and can lead to a very enthusiastic response from the salesman. Once the sales force realizes the broader responsibilities, they may well provide an essential and effective research role.

5.2 UTILIZING THE OUTSIDE CONSULTANT

Consultancies offer a wide variety of services. These vary from the large companies who are only interested in large-scale jobs to the one-man company offering his experience and expertise in a very limited field. It is possible, therefore, for the consultancy to offer all or any single part of the research programme. It is unlikely that the small company will ever be able to afford consultants for the whole of their work. A consultant charges amounts varying from £100 to £500 per day, depending on the skill and experience of the agency; it is possible to pay a cheaper rate but only when the consultant has some other sources of income; for example, junior college/polytechnic lecturers can charge as little as £50 per day.

The most crucial part of work with consultants is the briefing stage. This is often the make-or-break point of the survey. The brief should be written. There is often a great temptation to simply talk through the problem with the consultant and then leave him to come back with his proposals. Try to avoid this; it is sloppy and leads to carelessness. The company knows the problems better and realizes the implications as to how the research will be used. No company can abdicate its responsibility for the outcome, even if all or part of the work is being done by outsiders. It must be clearly understood that the ownership of the work belongs to the client. He works with the consultant, not against him. There is a tendency for companies to view the consultant in isolation; a person to be congratulated or blamed depending on the outcome. This view should be avoided.

The brief should outline precisely what information is required. Background information, definitions, specifications and constraints such as special factors and timing should be included. If field work only is required it is necessary to specify the number of interviews required, their location, duration and nature.

How to Choose a Consultant

Organizations such as IMRA (Industrial Market Research Association), MRS (Market Research Society), CBI (Confederation of British Industry) and BIM (British Institute of Management) will provide lists of consultants from amongst their members.

In addition, the Small Firms Information Service and the Industrial Liaison Officer network will provide local knowledge of consultants. The problem, then, is to decide who should be invited to quote. Perhaps the easiest way to solve this is to telephone a couple of research buyers in larger organizations to seek their advice. Be quite sure what is being sought in the following areas:

(1) Amount of involvement by consultancy;
(2) Experience required from consultant;
(3) Amount to be spent.

Researchers as a profession are very supportive and helpful to one another because, more than any other functional area within industry, they fully realize the importance of ensuring that all research conducted conforms to the codes of standard jointly published by IMRA/MRS. These standards must be maintained by all who are involved in research. Thus researchers in other companies have a vested interest in seeing that first-time clients do use legitimate consultancies. As in many professions, the market research industry has suffered from abuse by individuals and organizations disparagingly referred to as 'cowboys'. These organizations are likely to offer very cheap consultancy. Beware of them and consequently the cheapest quote.

Short-list about three companies and invite them to respond to the brief. Some companies may decline the invitation, but in doing so are likely to recommend another better-equipped source for consultancy. A face-to-face meeting between client and consultancy is highly beneficial. Apart from enabling the clarification of any ambiguities in the brief and the clearing of any problems, it allows the fostering of a *rapport* between the client and consultant.

In industrial markets there is a tendency to employ consultants with previous experience in the particular market sector under consideration. It is argued that the technical knowledge required necessitates the use of consultants with a field force familiar with the products, processes and jargon of the industry under consideration. Another school of thought would propound the view that, as well as offering the advantages outlined, a consultancy which has done it all before could find it extremely difficult to review the problem in a totally objective and uninhibited way. Edward de Bono[8] one of the leading authorities on creativity, argues that the fact that we have done something previously seriously limits our ability to look afresh at the problem on subsequent occasions.

Cost-comparisons

The most cost-effective method of carrying out any research will to a large extent depend upon the facilities and resources available to the company and the needs and requirements of the research undertaken.

We have previously assessed that to use in-company personnel to carry out research costs approximately £50 per day (see page 57). In the preparation of this book many market research agencies were contacted in order to assess the cost of using agency personnel to carry out the intended research. The costs quoted are not intended to be taken as verbatim but solely to give some idea of the costs involved:

(1) Consultant day, approximately £100–£200 per day;
(2) A group discussion, approximately £250–£800, depending on the length and manuscript provision;
(3) A specialist depth interviewer, approximately £40 per day excluding travelling;
(4) A general interviewer, approximately £30 per day.

The actual cost per interview is difficult to detail as it will differ substantially depending on the survey.

If a general interviewer is used for a telephone survey, then if thirty interviews are obtained in a day the interviewer cost can be as little as £1 per interview. Similarly, if personal interviews are conducted in one set location (i.e. street interviewing, where 30–40 can be carried out), the cost per interview can be very small. However, if the potential respondents are in different locations and travelling is involved, then it may be only possible to carry out five or six interviews, in which case the cost per interview is greatly increased.

The interviewing costs for group discussions again can vary greatly. If the transcript is long and involved and the group discussion has only four members, then the interview cost can be as much as £200 per interview. But at the other extreme, with a simple and clearly defined transcript and a larger group, costs can be greatly minimized.

It is important for any researcher to employ the most cost-effective method available to him. What this course is will primarily depend on his own judgement and the different options available to him for the successful completion of the survey.

5.3   MULTI-CLIENT STUDIES

Multi-client studies are normally available in two forms:

(1) (a) Where an agency identifies a research need and sponsors the work itself. The resulting report is made available to all interested parties at a fee;
    (b) Where a consultant identifies a need and obtains sponsors.

Several of these studies are continuous, such as the various audits involving panels of respondents. If fuller information is required contact:
The Market Research Society,
15 Belgrave Square,
London SW1X 8PF.

(2) This is where the initiative comes from a group of probably non-competing manufacturers with a common interest in a specific market. An example of this sort of multi-client study is the co-operation of:

   (a) A gas central heating boiler manufacturer;
   (b) A central heating control manufacturer;
   (c) A pipe manufacturer;
   (d) A pump distributor;
   (e) A radiator manufacturer.

These parties all have a specific interest in their own product and a general interest in the central heating market. A common survey is then agreed with, perhaps, opportunity for each contributor to ask specific questions. The resulting survey is obviously cost-effective.

One very significant advantage of a good multi-client survey is that a considerable *rapport* can develop between the consultancy and the participants as well as between the participants themselves. Thus, informal, reliable information passes between the group—an extremely effective method of obtaining good, authoritative market data.

5.4 CONCLUSION

This chapter has outlined the ways in which the research can be done. We have discussed the role of other in-company personnel, sales personnel as well as consultants and multi-client possibilities.

We have costed the various options and conclude that the best possible utilization of resources is:

(1) Plan and co-ordinate work internally.
(2) Use the sales force or an external field work agency for specific interviews.

Chapter 6

The Questionnaire

The questionnaire is probably the most crucial single element in the whole of the market research investigation. It is the vehicle for collecting the information required. The reader can be forgiven for expecting such an important area of work to be very well documented in literature, but in reality it is not.

In this chapter we will demonstrate the drafting of questionnaires of varying degrees of complexity by showing a series of examples of questionnaires that have been used. These examples are not meant to demonstrate the perfect questionnaire—we have still to find one! Rather they demonstrate layout, question construction and wording that have been used. The chapter opens with a series of widely accepted rules for questionnaire design and construction. Examples are given of the use of guarantee cards, non-question questionnaires (forms) and other longer and more sophisticated questionnaires.

It is assumed that the objectives of the questionnaire are absolutely clear to the questionnaire designer. Even so, time is well spent talking the questionnaire through with a potential or typical respondent and, where time permits, a pilot survey of two or three respondents should be undertaken.

6.1 DRAFTING THE QUESTIONNAIRE

There are normally four major parts of a formal questionnaire. Each part contains specific information. These are:

Identification of the Survey

This section should include the survey title and, where appropriate, the name of the company doing the study along with a survey number if confusion could possibly arise. The interviewer's identity and the conditions of the interview (i.e. time, weather, etc.) should be recorded.

Identification of the Respondent

This does not necessarily mean the name of the respondent but certainly it is important to identify the company, its size and production capabilities. The rank, status of the respondent and any special observed characteristics should be included in this section.

Control Questions

Control questions are designed to determine whether or not the respondent is giving consistent answers and, in the case of postal questionnaires, can determine whether the instructions for completing the questionnaire have been followed. The most common devices for control questions are:

(1) Asking a question twice in different parts of the questionnaire;
(2) Inserting bogus options into the questionnaire which would deceive an unknowledgable respondent, e.g. Which lifting gear does your company use?

> Crane
> Forklift truck
> Sky hook
> Block and tackle

Any sky hook responses would be questioned!
   Control questions are very helpful in the final stages of long interviews and can be used to identify the fatigue factor which, with the best will in the world from the respondent, creeps in when interviews extend beyond half an hour in length.

The Survey Questions

This is obviously the major part of the questionnaire and requires most attention. Before looking at those questions in greater detail two further major issues need resolving, namely:

(1) The length of the questionnaire; and
(2) The necessity for interviewers'/respondents' instructions.

6.2   LENGTH OF QUESTIONNAIRE

Figure 8 illustrates the optimum time limits for different forms of questionnaire surveys. Many eminent researchers will be able to point to extremely successful experience with surveys outside the time parameters listed. However in the authors' experience it is the opinion that Figure 8 will provide the reader with suitable guidelines on which to base his questionnaire design.

6.3   INSTRUCTIONS

A vital part of any questionnaire is to ensure that the instructions on the completion of the questionnaire are clear and unambiguous. Ensure that the respondent knows:

64

Postal questionnaire	Maximum of 20 questions
Telephone survey	Time limit 15 minutes
Face-to-face interview (in office/home)	Time limit 30 minutes
Face-to-face interview (street)	Time limit 3 minutes

Figure 8. Optimum time limits for questionnaire surveys

(1) Which questions to omit;
(2) How they are expected to respond: by a tick, by a cross, or writing down the answers.

6.4 TYPES OF QUESTIONS

There are four main question types:

(1) Simple dichotomous questions;
(2) Multi-choice questions;
(3) Open-ended questions;
(4) Scaling questions.

Dichotomous Questions

These are the simplest of questions to ask, as they are designed to be answered in only one of two possible ways. They are the basis of the sequential sampling method outlined in Chapter 4. For example,

(1) Does your company buy wire rod?

Yes	
No	

(2) Which of the two products A or B do you think is the most attractive?

A	
B	

The questions are easy to ask and analyse. But beware that the situation is truly a two-way choice. In our examples above 'Don't know' could well be a response to question 1 and neither or both to question 2.

Multi-choice Questions

Respondents are able to choose from a range of possible answers: for example

Where did you buy your trailer from?	Manufacturer	☐
	Merchant	☐
	Importer	☐
	Second-hand centre	☐
	Other (please name)	_____

Again these questions are very easy to analyse, but it is important that, wherever possible, all options are listed. Often an option you have never considered emerges. For this reason always include an option of other (please specify).

Open-ended Questions

These questions, known also as free answer or free response, calls for a wide variety of response. The topic is established for the respondent, who is then left to structure a reply as he sees fit. For example,
Why do you use plastic piping? . . . .
. . . .
Avoid these questions wherever possible: they are both difficult to record and analyse. Try to produce a multi-choice question.

There are, however, situations where only open-ended questions are appropriate, particularly when assessing attitudes and opinions.

Scaling Questions

Over recent years the academic world has spent much of its time reviewing questions where attitudes and other subjective evidence can be compiled. There are several devices that have now been used, and we will highlight two: Likert scales, and semantic differential.

Rensis Likert[9] developed a method of determining the weight of attitudinal response. A respondent is asked to what extent he agrees or disagrees with a particular statement indicating whether they

Strongly agree;
Agree;
Uncertain;
Disagree;
Strongly disagree.

These five categories are then scored, usually using 5, 4, 3, 2, 1 respectively; for example,

The sales of fan convectors will grow in the next 6 months

5 Strongly agree	4 Agree	3 Uncertain	2 Disagree	1 Strongly disagree

The sales of gas fires will drop in the next 6 months

5 Strongly agree	4 Agree	3 Uncertain	2 Disagree	1 Stongly disagree

Semantic Differentials

The semantic differential (Osgood, Suci and Tannerbaum, 1957)[10] is one of the most common scaling techniques in marketing research used to determine the views of the respondent as to the attributes of a particular product. Since its conception the original model has been modified and upgraded (Hughes 1975).[11] However, in comparability tests carried out by Evans (1980)[12] it was concluded that the original model took less time to complete and had a higher response rate than the later one. Hence the traditional semantic differential methodology will be discussed here.

Method

To test the respondent's attitude to specific product attributes he is first presented with a list of the attributes to be measured; for example, the image of Company X:

Measured Product Attributes

(1)   Overall reputation of supplier
(2)   Financing terms
(3)   Supplier's flexibility in adjusting to your company's needs
(4)   Experience with the supplier in analogous situations
(5)   Technical service offered
(6)   Confidence in the salesman
(7)   Convenience of placing the order
(8)   Data on reliability of the product
(9)   Price
(10)   Technical specifications
(11)   Ease of operation or use
(12)   Preferences of principal user of the product
(13)   Training offered by the supplier
(14)   Training time required
(15)   Reliability of delivery data promised
(16)   Ease of maintenance
(17)   Sales service expected after date of purchase.

The respondents are then asked to judge each attribute on a six-point scale with the following descriptive phrases:

Product attribute	Very important	Important	Somewhat important	Unimportant	Very unimportant
1					
.					
.					
.					
17					

On completion by the sample of respondents a profile of the attitudes can be drawn up. One of the main advantages of this method is that it can be very easily used to obtain attitudinal profiles of different products or different services, enabling easy comparison to be carried out.

6.5   DRAFTING THE QUESTIONS

The exact form and phrasing the questions will take will depend on the nature of the survey and the type of respondent. There are, however, some fundamental requirements for all good questionnaire design:

(1)   Make it as simple as possible, bearing in mind the subject matter;
(2)   Make it easy for the respondent;

(3) Do not digress—only ask pertinent questions;
(4) Bear the subsequent analysis in mind.

The following good habits should be adopted:

Each Question Should Cover One Point at a Time

An apparently simple question can prove to be tortuously involved. For example: Which supplier offers the best price and delivery? The respondent has the possible dilemma:

(1) All prices are the same;
(2) The best price has not the best delivery;
(3) What is 'best' anyway?

Questions Should be Unambiguous

The ambiguous question has no place in market research. Examples abound, many of them due to the imprecise nature of the English language. For example: Do you use block and tackle lifting gear? In this question the 'you' can refer to the individual or the company. The word 'use' is ambiguous; use could be interpreted as physical work or to have access to on a regular basis or to have access to on an irregular basis. When all other faults have been eliminated the persistent one of ambiguity generally remains.

Leading and Misleading Questions should be Avoided

'Don't you think that the lifting capacity is too small?' Such a question does not ask the respondent to think about an answer but suggests one to him. Unless he is particularly interested he will not wish to argue. Another common leading question is that which is more at home in an advertisement than a research study. For example: Would you say that X hand tools are preferred because of the company's accent on quality?

Good Sequencing and Question Flow

Start with simple questions which are easy to answer ensuring that the questions follow a logical progression. Flow and rhythm are often more important than grammatical correctness. Keep sensitive questions until the end of the questionnaire.

Don't Ask Unanswerable Questions

It is important to emphasize that a respondent can only answer questions about his own attitudes and experience. It is impossible to make far-seeing forecasts;

even though one is tempted, avoid questions such as

Do you think your competitors will react to the situation? What will be the sales of your boilers in five years' time? Do you expect to be market leaders? If product X were available would you buy it?

Some Further Points

Do not offend or embarrass;
Use prompt cards to help the respondent;
Vary the question types—do not be monotonous;
Use positive questions; negative questions should be avoided.

6.6   EXAMPLES OF QUESTIONNAIRES

Example 1: Local Authority Ticket Costs—A Comparative Survey

The following questionnaire, used for a postal survey, has been included here to give an example of bad design. As the reader will see on examination of the questionnaire:

(1)   There are no clear instructions; thus the respondent is totally unaware of what is expected of him;
(2)   It is quite formidable; far too much information is required at once;
(3)   It is too lengthy, requiring detailed knowledge of quite minor types of tickets;
(4)   There is no apparent logic to the layout of the questionnaire.

The net result would most likely be that, on receipt, the respondent would totally disregard it and decline replying.

Example 2: Survey of Visitors to 1977 Interbuild Exhibition

This example shows a questionnaire quite adequately designed to determine the viewpoints of visitors to an exhibition. As will be noticed, it is quite clear to the respondent what answers are expected of him and each question is relatively easy for the respondent to answer. It will also be of interest to note that the respondent was offered an incentive for completing the questionnaire.

Example 3: The Guarantee Card

The guarantee card is often overlooked as a basis for continuous marketing information. A little forethought, and the card can be used very effectively. This example is supplied by a gas fire manufacturer. Not only does it collect the information normally associated with the guarantee but it asks three very useful additional questions.

Example 1

Name of local authority . . . .

Department . . . .

TICKET RANGE	STYLE OF TICKET*				APPROXIMATE QUANTITIES* USED PER ANNUM					APPROX. COST PER 1000 TICKETS	APPROX. SIZE OF TICKET IF AVAILABLE
	Roll form	Single ticket	Specific wording	General wording	Under 10 000	10 001 to 100 000	100 001 to 250 000	250 001 to 500 000	Over 500 000		
Car Park Manual Use											
Car Park Automatic Dispenser											
Baths											
Tennis											
Golf											
Theatre											
Show											
Laundry											
Library											
School Meals											

Procedure	Annual Tender		Regular	Orders	Orders placed	Numbers of Suppliers				
	YES	NO	YES	NO	centrally / by user	1	2	3	4	5

In your opinion is there a trend towards general stock issue tickets as opposed to specific ranges?

YES	NO

*Please tick appropriate box and refer any queries to:

This questionnaire has been completed by: Name . . . .

Position . . . .

Example 2

Survey of Visitors to 1977 Interbuild Exhibition

1. Is this the first time that you have visited Interbuild?　　　　Yes ☐　　No ☐

2. Approx. how long in total did you spend at the exhibition?　　.................... hours

3. Before attending the exhibition which, if any, were the principal companies whose stands you intended to visit?

i ....　　ii ....

iii ....　　iv ....

4. Of all the stands you noticed, please try to name the 2 which attracted your attention the most and why.

Company	Reason why
....	....
....	....

5. Please indicate in the appropriate boxes below:-

　(a) Which of the following product groups are of interest to you, and

　(b) in which, if any, do you propose to change brands or use additional brands as a result of what you saw at the exhibition?

	(a) of Interest	(b) Change/add. Brands		(a) of Interest	(b) Change/add. Brands
Ceramic sanitaryware	☐	☐	Copper fittings:-	☐	☐
Shower cubicles/enclosures	☐	☐	- solder ring fittings	☐	☐
Showers:-	☐	☐	- end-feed fittings	☐	☐
- thermostatic mixing valves	☐	☐	- compression fittings	☐	☐
- blending valves	☐	☐	Radiator valves:-	☐	☐
- electric instantaneous heaters	☐	☐	- manual radiator valves	☐	☐
Baths:-	☐	☐	- thermostatic radiator valves	☐	☐
- acrylic baths	☐	☐	Microbore radiator valves	☐	☐
- cast iron baths	☐	☐	Plastic waste systems	☐	☐
- steel baths	☐	☐	Plastic rainwater & soil systems	☐	☐
Bath, basin & sink taps & mixers:-	☐	☐	Plastic underground drainage systems	☐	☐
- standard/economy ranges	☐	☐			
- luxury taps & mixers	☐	☐	All the above products	☐	☐

6. Which new products on display impressed you most?

New Product	Company
....	....
....	....
....	....
....	....
....	....

7. Without referring elsewhere, please try to identify the companies you associate with the following brand names:-

"Adelphi"	:	....	"Adriatic"	:	....
"Alterna"	:	....	"Aqualisa"	:	....
"Conex"	:	....	"Cosmos"	:	....
"Danum"	:	....	"Delcop"	:	....
"Domino"	:	....	"Idealblend"	:	....
"Mira"	:	....	"Peglertherm"	:	....
"Silver Spa"	:	....	"Tantara"	:	....

8. At which of the following stands did you stop (a) just to look, (b) to talk, or (c) to acquire literature? Where applicable, please indicate **how** helpful you found the stand personnel by inserting the following key in the space provided: (4) if very good; (3) if good; (2) if fair; (1) if **poor**; (x) if no one available to talk.

	(a) Just Looked	(b) Talked	(c) Literature	How Helpful		(a) Just Looked	(b) Talked	(c) Literature	How Helpful
E.G. XYZ Ltd.	☐	☑	☑	**(2)**	Key Terrain	☐	☐	☐	....
					Lawley Gaunt	☐	☐	☐	....
Armitage Shanks	☐	☐	☐	....	Marley	☐	☐	☐	....
Barking-Grohe	☐	☐	☐	....	Midland Metals	☐	☐	☐	....
Bartol Plastics	☐	☐	☐	....	Paragon Plastics	☐	☐	☐	....
Carron Co.	☐	☐	☐	....	Peglers	☐	☐	☐	....
Conex Sanbra	☐	☐	☐	....	Tantofex Engineers	☐	☐	☐	....
Deltaflow	☐	☐	☐	....	Twyfords	☐	☐	☐	....
Heatons Bathrooms	☐	☐	☐	....	Yorkshire Imperial Metals	☐	☐	☐	....
Ideal Standard	☐	☐	☐	....	Walker Crosweller	☐	☐	☐	....
IMI Opella	☐	☐	☐	....	Wavin/Osma	☐	☐	☐	....

9. What is the principal activity of your company/organisation?

....

....

10. Please indicate below the part you play within your Company/Organisation in the purchase of the following products:-

		No Part	Recommend	Specify	Final Decision
Bathroom products	:	☐	☐	☐	☐
Kitchen products	:	☐	☐	☐	☐
Plastic pipe and fittings	:	☐	☐	☐	☐
Plumber's brassware	:	☐	☐	☐	☐

11 Overall, what do you consider to be the most useful benefit gained from your visit to INTERBUILD '77 ?

....
....
....
....
....

12. Do you have any further comments?

....
....
....
....
....
....
....

- -

Name	:	....
Position	:	....
Company	:	....
Address	:	....
		....
		....

☐ *Please tick if you do **not** wish to receive a gift.*

Many thanks for your help

74

Example 3

Belmont

Date of installation _____

Name _____

Address _____

_____

_____ Post code _____

Supplier or
Installer _____

Address _____

_____

_____ Post code _____

Please tick the appropriate box

1 Is your house centrally heated?
Yes ☐   No ☐
If YES which fuel is used?
Gas ☐ Electricity ☐
Oil ☐ Solid Fuel ☐

2 When was your house built?
Pre 1918 ☐ 1918-38 ☐
1939-59 ☐ 1960-79 ☐

3 Does your Baxi Belmont replace another fire?
Yes ☐   No ☐
If YES, what type of fire was it?
Gas fire   ☐
Electric Fire   ☐
Solid Fuel Open
                        Fire ☐

If after 1979, please state date built _____

IMPORTANT — Please complete and return this card and register this Guarantee.

Example 4

An excellent example of a good form is your income tax return. Next year take special note and enjoy completing it!

Chapter 7

International Marketing Research

In carrying out research on an international scale, the basic format detailed in earlier chapters will equally apply here. Although the basic elements of the

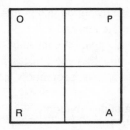

research programme will be similar, any marketing research on an international scale will have more than its share of difficulties. These may be due to the following factors:

(1) The researcher's lack of familiarity with the foreign market.
(2) The lack of assistance of reliable statistical data.
(3) Lack of co-operation due to the country's unfamiliarity with marketing research.
(4) The large commitment required by the company both in personnel and financial resources.
(5) The difficulties of coping with a different language and a different culture.

Because of these difficulties, if the company is to carry out effective international field research it is important that it has the expertise within the company to carry out the task and also large resources to draw upon to finance the project. It is unlikely that the small company has such resources, but this does not mean it is unable to research foreign markets effectively.

The importance of secondary information has already been stressed in Chapter 2. In international research the collection of secondary information is of crucial importance and often the most cost-effective method of researching. It is for this reason that the objective of this chapter is to give the researcher a practical guide to the information sources available within the UK for international markets; and provide a guide to the organizations that will readily give advice and help to the researcher involved in international marketing research.

7.1 INFORMATION NEEDS

As in any research, before the search for information begins it is necessary to think clearly about the problem in hand and draw up a list of information needs together with a list of possible sources of information. In the booklet *How to Start Exporting* published by the Small Firms Division of the Department of Trade, a market checklist of factors to be considered in international market research is given. It is well worth repeating here:

International market checklist

Approximate size of the market (production, imports, exports).
Political/economic stability of the market.
Growth trends (production and apparent consumption).
Products currently available (how they meet tastes, habits, etc).
Leading competitors, market shares, promotion methods, services and facilities offered.
Channels of distribution, cost of distribution.
Legal requirements, standards, etc.
Tariffs, quotas, import licences.
Ease of transportation (speed, frequency of services, cost).
Product subject to official technical regulations or standards.

To the small firm, the task of obtaining such information may seem formidable. The rest of this chapter will discuss the various methods by which the above information can be obtained from sources that are readily available. These sources can be divided into the following categories:

International statistical sources;
Public sources of information;
Commercial sources of information.

7.2 INTERNATIONAL STATISTICAL SOURCES

International Publications

Any researcher involved in the examination of international statistics will find the sources quite extensive. The major problem one encounters is the comparability of the data. It is because of the problem of comparability of statistical information that it will be necessary for the researcher to grasp quickly the intricacies of the major classification systems in order to understand what is contained in the data under analysis.

There are a number of international trade classifications, some major ones being the following:

(1) Brussels Tariff Nomenclature (BTN);
(2) Standardized Industrial Trade Classification (SITC). This is a four-digit code of 625 sub-groups covering all commodities and all goods moving in world trade;
(3) 'INTERFILE.' This is operated by the World Trade Centre, New York and is broken down into three categories:

Function/subject;
Country code;
SITC (revised version).

Most international publications have made much progress in the conformity of the classification of data. Thus before embarking on an investigation of the national statistics of a country it is advisable to examine statistics from an international source. Although these may not be as detailed as national statistics, they are normally more uniform and objective and provide a useful starting-point.

The following publishing bodies provide excellent information on an international scale:

European Economic Community (EEC);
European Coal and Steel Community;
Economic Commission for Africa (ECA);
Economic Commission for Asia and the Far East (ECAFE);
Economic Commission for Latin America (ECLA);
Organization for Economic Co-operation and Development (OECD);
General Agreement on Tariffs and Trade (GATT);
Food and Agriculture Organization (FAO);
International Labor Organization (ILO);
International Civil Aviation Organization (ICAO);
International Bank for Reconstruction and Development (BRD);
International Monetary Fund (IMF);
International Telecommunications Union (ITU);
International Union of Railways (UICF);
International Air Transport Association (IATA);
Universal Postal Union (UPU);
World Health Organization (WHO).

Other useful sources of international information are:

Business International;
Informations Internationales;
World Trade Information Service—The US Department of Commerce.

Contact

(1) The Statistics and Marketing Intelligence Library,
1 Victoria Street
London SW1H 0ET.
Telephone 01-215 5444/5
(2) The local library, which will hold the majority of statistics published by the above international organizations.

National Statistics

As in the UK, in most countries the government is the major compiler, analyser and publisher of national statistics, but the method of collecting, storing and disseminating statistics varies greatly from country to country. Thus it would be impossible in this chapter to discuss the statistics available in each country. However, much work has been carried out on statistical sources, and it is hoped the following guides will aid the reader in obtaining the necessary national statistics:

(1) The British Overseas Trade Board in its series *Hints to Exporters* lists the basic statistical titles of the country concerned.
(2) The Statistics and Market Intelligence Library, Export House, holds the latest published statistics on many subjects from countries who issue them.
(3) Some useful guides on National statistics are the following:
Statistics Africa, Joan M. Harvey
Statistics America, Joan M. Harvey
Statistics Europe, Joan M. Harvey
Statistics Asia and Australasia, Joan M. Harvey
(all published by CBD Research)
Compendium of Sources: Basic Commodity Statistics, GATT
Bibliography of Industrial and Distributive Trade Statistics, United Nations
National Statistical Publications, United Nations

7.3 PUBLIC INFORMATION SOURCES

British Overseas Trade Board (BOTB)

The BOTB offers a host of services and facilities to the would-be exporter. In this section we are primarily concerned with the services offered to the export market researcher.

Export Marketing Research Scheme (EMRS)

The EMR is open to all exporters or potential exporters whose goods and services are produced in the UK, with priority being given to applicants with little or no experience of export marketing research.

The services provided are as follows:

(1) Free advice on the best methods of conducting research in overseas markets. This advice is given by professional market researchers employed by the BOTB.

(2) Financial support in the carrying out of overseas research projects:

    (a) In approved *ad hoc* projects carried out by a research consultant the BOTB will provide up to one third of the research costs incurred to individual companies;

    (b) For approved in-house research projects, support is normally 50% of overseas travel and subsistence costs necessarily incurred in the course of the research, provided that the BOTB is satisfied that the research ability of the applicant is comparable to that of professional agencies.

Contact

For full information of the scheme contact BOTB, Export Marketing Research, 1, Victoria Street, London SW1.
Telephone: 01-215 5216

The Export Intelligence Service (EIS)

This computer-based service provides subscribers with a wide range of selective export information, including details of specific export opportunities, calls for tender, market reports, changes in tariffs, import regulations, etc.

Contact

EIS at Lime Grove, Eastcote, Ruislip, Middlesex, Telephone: 01-868-1422 or the export section of your nearest BOTB regional office.

Cost

A charge of £45 is made for 150 notices, which means each item of intelligence will cost around 30p.

The International Directory of Published Market Research

This very useful directory, published by the BOTB, gives details of market research reports available to the public that have been carried out on a number of subjects in a variety of countries. The directory is indexed by commodities and cross-referenced by country. A brief resumé of each report itemized is given. Thus it is very easy for the researcher to ascertain whether the research of his interest has previously been carried out and is available in a published form.

Contact

Arlington Management Publications, 87, Germain Street, London. Telephone: 01-930-3638.

Cost

The directory can be purchased for a price of £18.95.

7.4 LIBRARIES

Statistics and Market Intelligence Library

This library has previously been mentioned in Section 7.2. It is included here due to the extensive amount of published information it has available on overseas markets. An inspection of the material available here will save the researcher much time and money. Further to the large amount of statistics the library holds the following sources of information can also be found:

(1) A large selection of international foreign trade and telephone directories.
(2) An extensive collection of capital development plans from all over the world providing the earliest possible indication of possible export opportunities.
(3) Many overseas business reports and market reports published by, for example, the US Department of Commerce.
(4) The library also subscribes to a number of indexing and abstracting services, e.g. *Middle East Data File Index* and a number of predicast services, including *Worldcasts*.

Contact

As in section 7.2.

Other Commercial Libraries

Many business and commercial libraries throughout the UK hold directories and commercial information useful to the exporter, and it is recommended that such a library would be a useful initial starting-point for the export market researcher.

Contact

Your local library. The Warwick University Library has an excellent international service. It holds a range of international statistical information and foreign directories as well as commercial information of international enterprises.

Contact

See page 29, Chapter 2.

7.5 TECHNICAL HELP TO EXPORTERS (THE)

THE is an offshoot of the British Standards Institution, who in the past few years have steadily built up a commercial information service for the exporter based on the information to be found in standards, regulations and codes of foreign standards organizations and on the detailed knowledge of commercial requirements collected by THE engineers.

The main value of THE to the market researcher is the provision of the following services:

(1) The library, which contains a unique collection of over 18 000 documents covering information from over 160 countries;
(2) The enquiry service, which is operated specifically to deal with day-to-day problems of the exporter and therefore designed to deal with the quick enquiry which is often answerable over the telephone.

Contact

Technical Help to Exporters BSI, Maylands Avenue, Hemel Hempstead, Hertfordshire HP2 4SQ. Telephone: Hemel Hempstead 3111.

Cost

The fees charged for the services depends on the particular service used, the complexity of the enquiry and whether or not you are a member of THE. Certain services are not available to non-members, e.g. the use of library facilities.

7.6 EMBASSIES

A useful starting-point of an investigation may be the embassy of that country, as most embassies have commercial departments with commercial information on their countries. However, it must be remembered that the most important commercial function of an embassy is to help their nationals to sell abroad, rather than help foreigners to sell into the countries they represent. The British Embassy of the country abroad may therefore be a more useful contact and should be initially approached through the local BOTB Office.

7.7 COMMERCIAL SOURCES OF INFORMATION

National Exporters' Associations/Trade Associations

National exporters' associations and trade associations (previously referred to in Chapter 2) can often be found to be a valuable aid to the international marketing researcher. They are generally organized on an industry or trade basis and effectively represent the national interests of their members. As such they can offer the following services to the researcher:

(1) The sponsoring and undertaking of overseas marketing research on an industry basis, making the findings and recommendations available to subscribing members only.

(2) Sponsored research by an association can qualify for financial support under the Export Marketing Research Scheme of the BOTB. In fact, many associations have undertaken successful joint ventures with the BOTB.

(3) Associations generally have many international contacts. Thus if the association is not able to help, it may well be able to direct the researcher to the relevant source.

(4) Provision of export intelligence and opportunities.

Contact

See page 26, Chapter 2.

Cost

See page 26, Chapter 2.

7.8 CHAMBERS OF COMMERCE

The services of chambers of commerce, as discussed in Chapter 2, do vary throughout the country. However, at a national level chambers of commerce undertake trade missions abroad, often in collaboration with trade associations, and so can be found to be a useful source of information and overseas contacts.

At an international level the International Chamber of Commerce can bring together producers, manufacturers and traders, consumers and bankers from over seventy countries in order to 'pool experience and forego a common policy adapted to both national and international requirements'. The major objectives of the International Chamber of Commerce are to:

Promote business interests at an international level;
Foster the greater freedom of international trade;
Harmonize and facilitate business and trade practices.

As such, the ICC can be a valuable source to the researcher wishing to establish overseas contacts. Further to this, the ICC operates an extensive research and publications service, having published in booklet form many reports which may be of topical interest to the exporter.

Contact

Your local chamber of commerce for further details or the International Chamber of Commerce, British National Committee, 6 Dean Farrar Street, London SW1. Telephone: 01-222 3755.

7.9   THE *FINANCIAL TIMES* BUSINESS INFORMATION SERVICE

The *Financial Times* Business Information Service, as well as being a valuable source of information to the UK researcher, can be effective as an aid to the researcher investigating international markets. In addition to the services detailed in Chapter 2, the following are provided:

1) Disclosure—American Company Information. Through this service the *Financial Times* has immediate access to information covering all the 12 000-plus publicly quoted companies registered with the US Securities and Exchange Commission. The reports cover details of a company's structure and activities, its properties, the number of its equity security holders, its sales and income and details of its directors. All the reports are held on microfiche, which makes for easy handling and reading.
2) The *Financial Times* Information Service has access to most international published statistics, e.g. all statistics published by such bodies as the OECD, UN, EEC and IMF, and in fact has a terminal for accessing databases such as the above, enabling the speedy provision of the required data.

Contact

The *Financial Times* Business Information Services. See page 24, Chapter 2.

Cost

See page 24, Chapter 2.

7.10   THE LONDON WORLD TRADE CENTRE

There are now eighteen fully operational world trade centres throughout the world, and any member of the London Centre can have the advantage of the expertise and contacts available through the worldwide network of world trade centres.

The main function of the trade centres is the provision of services and facilities, generally under the same roof. The facilities include general forms of assistance, e.g. translations, telex and secretarial and more specialized functions. One function of prime interest to this chapter is the Research and Information Department. This department keeps a comprehensive up-to-date commercial library including a trade-oriented press-cutting section. The projects undertaken by the department are many and diverse, including the following:

1) The provision of trade contacts;
2) The carrying-out of market research surveys;
3) The locating and screening of companies for clients with investment interests;

84

(4) The provision of a retainer service to keep clients informed on particula areas of interest by constant coverage of information sources.

Contact

World Trade Centre, London E1 9AA. Telephone: 01-488 2400.

Cost

For UK companies a joining fee of £50 is made plus annual subscriptions of £100.

It is worth noting that, whilst library services are available to everyone members will have the additional advantage of having the Research and Information Departments in the worldwide network of the trade centres at their disposal.

7.11 EXPORT-FACILITATING AGENCIES

At the national level there are many associations representing the interests of the British exporter that the researcher may find a profitable source of both expertise and information. These organizations provide a range of services and expertise which can provide a basis for research in export. The reader may find the following addresses useful:

(1) The International Exporters Association, PO Box 1, Bourne, Lincolnshire Telephone: 07782 3528.
(2) The British Export Houses Association, 69 Cannon Street, London N5AB Telephone: 01-248 4444.
(3) The British Federation of Commodity Associations, Plantation House Mincing Lane, London EC3M 3HT. Telephone: 01-626 1745.
(4) Manufacturers' Agents Association of Great Britain and Ireland, Inc., PO Box 9, Majestic House, Staines, Middlesex TW18 4DS. Telephone: Staines 53143.

7.12 US DEPARTMENT OF COMMERCE: NATIONAL TECHNICAL INFORMATION SERVICE (NTIS)

The National Technical Information Service of the US Department of Commerce is the central source for the public sale of US and foreign government-sponsored research, development and engineering reports and other analyses prepared by national and local governmental agencies and by special technology groups. The service basically acts as a clearing-house for scientific, technical and engineering information. Its information collection exceeds over one million titles, all of which are available for sale.

More pertinent to the reader will be the international market survey report service operated by NTIS. The NTIS have available international market survey reports and market share reports covering specialized industrial subjects in over a hundred countries throughout the world.

Contact

For full details and catalogues of available reports contact NTIS, United Kingdom Service Centre, PO Box 3, Newman Lane, Alton, Hampshire. Telephone 0420 84300.

Cost

There is no subscription charge for services provided. Each report is priced on an individual basis. These prices are seen to be very reasonable and can be very good value for money.

7.13 CONCLUSION

The objective of this chapter was to illustrate to the reader that in order to carry out marketing research on an international scale extortionate costs do not necessarily have to be incurred. Without having set foot on foreign soil there is a considerable amount of information which is readily available to the researcher if only he is able to find it. The sources outlined in this chapter should be able to guide the researcher to the relevant source for his particular research.

Further to this, in today's business environment much support is given by both government and commercial organizations in order to encourage the small firm to export. Such organizations can be of immense value to the researcher, not only in the help sometimes forthcoming in the way of financial support of a research project but also in the wealth of expertise and experience that these organizations have within their ranks. The company with little or no experience of marketing research in international markets may find that both time and money could be saved by making contact with these organizations rather than embarking on the project on his own.

Appendix 1: Code of Conduct

Introduction

This abridged version of the Code of Conduct of the Industrial Marketing Research Association and the Market Research Society applies to all forms of market and social research equally including, for instance, consumer surveys, psychological research, industrial surveys, observational studies, and panel research.

It is to be noted that the Industrial Marketing Research Association and the Market Research Society are bodies of individuals. Where the Code refers to organizations, such as client companies or research agencies, it is incumbent on individual members in these organizations to ensure, to the best of their ability, that the organization fulfils the Code in this respect. (Guidance on this point is given to members in Part VI of this Code.) In this Code the distinction has been drawn between 'Rules of conduct', which are mandatory and 'Good practice', which is recommended to members. These latter are items which the professional body wishes its members to follow when relevant but, because they cannot be formulated precisely for all circumstances, or it is recognized that members may not be able to adhere to them strictly on every single occasion, or they may not always be completely appropriate, or it is, as yet, premature to make them mandatory, the professional body does not feel it right to insist on their universal application. This does not mean that good practice is necessarily less important than the rules of conduct in a particular case and attention is drawn to Clause 1.5.

Definitions

For the purposes of this Code:

An informant

Is an individual person who provides information, either directly or indirectly, on which the results of a research project could, in whole or in part, be based.

An interview

Is any form of contact intended to provide such information, with such an informant.

86

The identity of an informant

Includes, as well as his name and/or address, any other information which offers a reasonable chance that he can be identified by any of the recipients of the information.

Records

Shall be deemed to include anything containing data whether primary as, for example, completed questionnaires or intermediate as, for example, computer print out. Besides the above, examples of records are interviewer schedules, self-completion sheets, tick lists and observational sheets, documents designed to be optically scanned, interviewer notes on semi-structured and unstructured interviews, tape recordings, photographs or films, video tapes, transcription sheets, edge punched cards and other forms of computer input, together with any documents necessary for their interpretation, e.g., coding and editing instructions.

Client

Shall be deemed to include any individual, organization, department, or division—including any belonging to the same organization as the research agency—which is reponsible for commissioning a research project.

Research agency

Shall be deemed to include any individual, organization, department, or division, including any belonging to the same organization as the client, which is responsible for conducting, or acting as a consultant on, a research project.

Where two or more individuals, organizations, departments, or divisions are together concerned in commissioning or conducting a research project, they shall be jointly and severally responsible for the observance of this Code of Conduct.

Overseas research

Where research is carried out overseas, Parts I, IV, V, and VI of the Code apply. As in the UK it shall be the duty of members in agencies specifically to point out to their clients any variation from the Standard Conditions in Part III. Where the codes of local market research societies or the equivalent are registered with the professional body, members must observe any responsibilities to informants that are set out in them; in any case, they must observe all the provisions in either Part II of this Code of Conduct or Section III A of the Code of the International Chamber of Commerce.

PART I: CONDITIONS OF MEMBERSHIP

1.1 The acceptance of market and social research depends upon the confidence of the business community and other users, and of the general public, in the integrity of practitioners. Members of the professional body undertake to refrain from any activity likely to impair such confidence and to comply with whatever general professional Code of Conduct, other regulations and interpretations may be laid down from time to time by the professional body.

It is important to this end that members should consider at all times that the purpose of market and social research is the collection and analysis of information, and not the direct creation of sales nor the influencing of the opinions of informants. It is in this spirit that this Code of Conduct has been devised.

1.2 Membership of the professional body is granted to individuals who are believed, on the basis of the information they have given, to have the required qualifications. Memberships may be withdrawn if this information is found to be inaccurate.

1.3 Membership may be withdrawn, or other disciplinary action taken, if, on the investigation of a complaint by anyone properly having access to a study, it is found that, in the opinion of the professional body, any important part of the work falls short of reasonable professional standards.

1.4 Membership may be withdrawn, or other disciplinary action taken, if a member is deemed guilty of unprofessional conduct. This is defined as a member:

(a) Misrepresenting himself as having qualifications, or experience, or access to facilities which he does not, in fact, possess.

(b) Being guilty of any act or conduct which, in the opinion of the Council, might bring discredit on the professional body or its members.

(c) Disclosing to any other person, firm, or company any information acquired in confidence during the course of his work regarding the business of a client, without the permission of that client.

(d) Having a receiving order made against him or making any arrangement or composition with his creditors.

(e) Being sentenced to a term of imprisonment by a Court of Law.

(f) Publishing, or otherwise disseminating, unjustified and unreasonable criticism of another member's work.

(g) Being guilty of any breach of the Rules of Conduct set out in subsequent parts of this document.

(h) Knowingly being in breach of any other regulations laid down from time to time by the Council of the professional body.

1.5 Failure to follow the good practice recommendations contained in subsequent parts of this Code shall not in itself constitute unprofessional conduct, but it may be taken into account by the Council when investigating a complaint against a member or when considering disciplinary action under any of the foregoing articles of this Code.

1.6 The Council will consider complaints in the light of the available evidence. It is empowered to call for such evidence from its members as seems necessary to investigate a complaint fairly. Membership may be withdrawn, or other disciplinary action taken, if a member should fail, without good reason, to assist the Council with its enquiries concerning a complaint against another member.

The Council may also request any evidence which seems necessary from non-members of the professional body. No member will have his membership withdrawn, or other disciplinary action taken under this Code, without an opportunity of a hearing before the Council, of which he shall have at least one month's notice.

PART II: RESPONSIBILITIES TO INFORMANTS

Preamble

The general principle on which the following Rules of Conduct are based is that informants are to be protected by members in the following ways:

(a) by having assurances honoured,
(b) by being allowed to remain anonymous,
(c) by avoiding any adverse effects from the contact,
(d) by being able to refuse or withdraw from an interview at any stage,
(e) by being able to check the credentials of the interviewer.

Rules of conduct

To ensure the protection set out above, the following rules will be honoured by members:

2.1 Any statement or assurance given to an informant in order to obtain cooperation shall be factually correct and honoured.

2.2 Subject to the provisions of this Clause, and those of Clause 2.7, the informant shall remain entirely anonymous.

No information obtained about individual informants which includes their identity shall be revealed, either directly or indirectly, other than to persons engaged in the administration, checking, or processing of research in accordance with this Code.

No information obtained about individual informants which includes their identity shall be used, either directly or indirectly, other than for the administration, checking, or processing of such research.

Information about individual informants which includes their identity shall only be further revealed to, or used by:

(a) Persons requiring it in order to conduct or process further interviews, after the first, with the same informants—subject to the conditions in Clause 2.6.
(b) Persons requiring it for other purposes, provided informants have consented to their identity being revealed, after being told the general purpose(s) of this revelation and the general nature of the recipient(s).

The member responsible for the research project must ensure that persons receiving such information are themselves bound by this Code of Conduct, or agree to abide by it for this purpose. (See also Good Practice Clause 2.8.)

2.3 All reasonable precautions shall be taken to ensure that the informant, and others closely associated with him, are, as individuals, in no way embarrassed, or adversely affected, as a direct result of any interview or interviews, including product test participation, or of any other communication concerning the research project. (See also Good Practice Clauses 2.10 and 2.14.)

2.4 The informant's right to withdraw, or to refuse to cooperate at any stage, shall be respected, unless the enquiry is being conducted under statutory powers. No procedure or technique which infringes this right shall be used, except that of observing or recording the actions or statements of individuals without their prior consent. In such a case the individual must be in a situation where he could reasonably expect his actions and/or statements to be observed and/or overheard (though not necessarily to be filmed or recorded). In addition at least one of the following conditions shall be observed:

(a) All reasonable precautions are taken to ensure that the individual's anonymity is preserved. (See also Good Practice Clause 2.10.)

(b) The individual is told immediately after the event that his actions and/or statements have been observed or recorded or filmed, is given the opportunity to see or hear the relevant section of the record and, if he wishes, to have it destroyed or deleted.

2.5 Members shall do their best to ensure that, on request at the time of the interview, the informant is provided with:

(a) an assurance that the interview is part of a research project (see also Clause 5.5).

(b) the information that the work is carried out under this Code (if necessary explaining the ways in which this protects informants).

(c) the name of the interviewer.

(d) the name of the responsible member of the professional body, and

(e) before the close of the interview, the name and address of the organization conducting the survey.

These statements may, if preferred, be shown in writing to the informant, e.g. on a card. Members should also do their best to provide the above information if the request is made after the close of the interview. (See also Good Practice Clause 2.11.)

Where the design of a postal survey necessitates the use of an accommodation address, arrangements shall be made for informants to discover, after its completion and if they should so wish, the name of the responsible member of the professional body, and the name and address of the organization conducting the survey.

Ownership of 'cover' organizations, when not separately registered with the Department of Trade and Industry, shall be registered with the professional body.

2.6 Further interviews, after the first, shall only be sought with the same informants under one or more of the following conditions:

(a) if informants' permission has been obtained at a previous interview, or

(b) if it is pointed out to informants that this interview is consequent upon one they have previously given and they then give their permission before the collection of further data, or

(c) if it is essential to the research technique involved that informants do not realize that this interview is consequent upon one they have previously given, but they do give their permission before the collection of further data—as though this were a new interview.

In all cases, the member responsible for the original interview must ensure, or receive assurances, that such further interviews are themselves conducted in accordance with this Code of Conduct. (See also Good Practice Clause 2.12.)

2.7 Where informants represent an organization, or are speaking for a function (e.g. marketing manager, managing director, etc.), then their organization may be listed in the report. It shall not, however, be possible for any particular piece of information obtained directly from an informant or otherwise provided in confidence to be related to any particular organization, nor for any individual informant to be identified, either directly or indirectly, except with prior permission from the relevant informant. This permission shall be sought before the relevant information is collected and the informant shall be informed of the extent to which it will be communicated. (See also Good Practice Clause 2.13.)

Good practice

In conjunction with the above rules of conduct, it is considered good practice:

2.8 For interviewers, coders, field office staff, and other persons who may see completed questionnaires or schedules containing informants' identities, to be aware of the contents of this Code and to have signed a statement to abide by the relevant sections. (See Rule of conduct 2.2.)

2.9 To be as open with informants as is practicable, either before the event or as soon as possible after it, about aspects of the research procedures that might concern them, such as the use of tape recorders, the nature of outside observers, etc.

2.10 When considering whether a research procedure would be permissible under Clauses 2.3 or 2.4, to remember that informants can be embarrassed not only by what has actually happened to them but also by what they can reasonably think may have happened or might happen. Such factors as the following should be taken into account:

(i)   the subject of the research.

(ii) the informant's likely assessment of the possibility of his being identified.

(iii) the relationship between the informant and those he is concerned might be able to identify him.

(iv) whether the likely identification of the informant is as an individual or merely as a member of a particular organization, and

(v)   the type or record used for the study.

2.11 Where possible and appropriate, for

(i)   statements and assurances given before the interview to cover
  (a) the nature of the survey and
  (b) the length of the interview (minimum and maximum likely duration).

(ii) at least items (c) and (e) in Clause 2.5 to be left with the informant in writing after the interview, and

(iii) the informant to be told, on request, the reasons for asking personal questions.

2.12 When seeking further interviews, after the first, with the same informants, to bear in mind that procedure (a) in Clause 2.6 is the one least likely to cause annoyance or give offence.

2.13 When interviewing representatives of companies or other organizations:

(a) To make appointments for interviews in advance.

(b) If discursive interviews are used, for an exchange of information to take place, and not to use personal interviews to obtain a basic understanding of the subject where such an understanding could have been obtained through desk research, etc.

(c) For the nature and/or the sponsor of the survey to be revealed where use of the information that will be contained in the survey report might have an adverse effect directly on the informant's company (e.g. when interviewing a competitor or a potential competitor). The provisions of Clause 3.2 shall, however, still be observed. (See also Rule of conduct 2.7.)

2.14 For everything possible to be done by the member and the interviewer to ensure a continuing climate of goodwill, responsibility, and trust. A meticulous standard of good manners should be maintained and everything should be done to leave the informant disposed to receive a future contact on another research project. (See also Rule of Conduct 2.3 and Clause 6.5.)

PART III: MUTUAL RESPONSIBILITIES WITHIN THE PROFESSION

The Mutual Responsibilities of Members from Client Companies and Research Agencies (or other members who use and supply research information or facilities)

A The relationship between a client and a research agency, or other research practitioner, will frequently be subject to a form of contract between them. This Code does not aim to limit the freedom of the parties to make whatever agreement they wish between themselves, provided that neither party shall be required to act in breach of any of the mandatory sections of this Code.

B In the absence of any agreement to the contrary, the following Standard Conditions shall govern the behaviour of client and agency. Furthermore, it shall be the duty of members in agencies specifically to point out to their clients any variation from these Standard Conditions.

Standard Conditions

3.1 Research specifications provided by a client, and proposals provided by an agency at the request of a client when the agency receives neither the commission nor payment for the proposals, remain the property of the client or agency respectively and their contents may not be revealed to third parties without permission. Cost quotations may, however, be revealed, so long as an individual quotation cannot be associated with a given research agency. (See also Good Practice Clause 3.12.)

3.2 Unless authorised to do so by the client, or instructed by a Court of Law, the research agency shall not reval to informants, nor to any other person not directly concerned with the work of the study, the identity of the client commissioning the study. (See also Clause 2.13(c).)

3.3 All confidential material relating to clients, including the fact that they have undertaken, or have considered undertaking, research in a particular area, shall remain confidential to persons wholly or substantially engaged in the service of the research agency. Whenever the client has reason to suppose that, due to any change of control or direction of the agency, or to other circumstances, any person not wholly or substantially engaged in the service of the agency may have access to confidential material relating to the client, the client may require possession of any such material held by the agency notwithstanding Clause 3.8. (See also Good Practice Clause 3.13.)

3.4 If fieldwork is to be subcontracted to another agency the client shall be so informed before being committed to the project.

3.5

(a) When two or more projects are combined in one interview, or the same project is carried out on behalf of more than one client, each client concerned shall be informed of this fact before being committed to the project. (See also Clauses 3.10 and 3.12.)

(b) Research agencies shall take all reasonable precautions to ensure that interviewers do not combine two or more projects in one interview without permission from themselves.

3.6 The research agency shall provide to the client, whether in the report proposals or elsewhere:

(a) A copy of the questionnaire or other schedule used (or, in the case of a shared project, that portion relating to the matter reported upon) and any relevant extract from interviewers' instructions, etc.

(b) An adequate description of the following:

    (i) For whom and by whom the study was conducted.

    (ii) The objects of the study.

    (iii) The universe covered (actual, not just intended).

    (iv) The size and nature of the sample and details of any weighting methods used: where applicable, the planned sample as well as the number of interviews actually achieved.

(v) The method of recruitment used for informants in qualitative research or other techniques involving prior recruitment of informants.

(vi) Weighted or unweighted bases for all conventional tables, clearly distinguishing between the two.

(vii) Where appropriate, and especially in the case of postal surveys, a statement of response rates and a discussion of possible bias due to non-response.

(viii) The method by which the information was collected (e.g. by personal interview, postal questionnaire, mechanical recording device, or some other method).

(ix) If any incentive offers were made to informants such as members of group discussions the details of the incentives and the stage at which they were offered and provided should be made clear.

(x) The time at which any fieldwork was done.

(xi) The field force and any field quality control methods used.

(xii) The names of any subcontractors used for major parts of the research.

(xiii) In the case of desk research, the sources used. (See also Clause 3.14.)

3.7 On request the client, or his mutually acceptable representative, may attend a limited number of interviews to observe the standard of the fieldwork (he then becomes subject to the provisions of Clause 2.2). In the case of multi-client surveys, the agency may require that the observer is independent of any of the clients. The agency is entitled to be recompensed if the client's desire to attend an interview interferes with, delays, or increases the cost of the field work.

3.8 Completed records shall be the property of the research agency (but see Clause 3.9). The agency shall be entitled to destroy such records without reference to the client two years, but no sooner, after the end of the fieldwork.

3.9 After the research agency has submitted its report upon the study to the agreed specification, the client shall be entitled to obtain from the research agency the original records, or duplicate copies of them, relating to his report, provided that the client shall bear the reasonable cost of preparing such records in a permissible form, and that the request is made within the time limit set by Clause 3.8. Such records shall not reveal the identity of informants, unless one of the conditions in Clause 2.2 or 2.6 has been fulfilled.

3.10 Unless the prior consent of the client has been obtained, any findings deriving from the study, other than published information, shall not be disclosed at any time by the research agency to any person other than to the client commissioning the study. This refers only to studies exclusively commissioned by a specific client, or clients, and it does not refer to the research techniques used in the study, nor to methodological analyses, so long as there is no disclosure of any such findings.

3.11 Reports, and other records or documents relevant to the project provided by a research agency, are normally for use within the client company or its associated companies (including the client's marketing, advertising and other relevant and duly authorised consultants or advisers), or other previously nominated recipients. If the client intends a wider circulation of the results of a study, either in whole or in part, the research agency's name may not be quoted in connection with the study until:

(a) it has approved the exact form and contents of the publication or circulation and

(b) it has agreed with the client which items under Clauses 3.6 and 3.14 may be provided by the agency to recipients of this wider circulation, on request and at the enquirer's expense if necessary. (See also Clauses 3.16, 5.3 and 5.6.)

Good practice

It is good practice for:

3.12 The terms and conditions under which research is undertaken to be defined as precisely and thoroughly as possible in a proposal, tender, or quotation submitted and approved before work is put in hand. This should include as many of the items listed under 3.6 and 3.14 as are relevant and also should state for example: if, and over what period, work on the same subject will not be carried out for a competitor without advance permission from the client (unless this is stated specifically, the client does not have the right to exclusive use of an agency); whether the client's identity may or may not be revealed to informants; if any subcontractors are to be used for major parts of the project and, if so, their identitities; if the project is not to be exclusive to the client (unless this is stated specifically it is assumed to be exclusive—see Clauses 3.5 and 3.10); and the ownership of the copyright (see also Standard Condition 3.1).

3.13 The research agency to take reasonable steps to ensure the security of reports, questionnaires, and other material which is confidential to any client. (See also Standard Condition 3.3.)

3.14 The research agency to provide to the client, in the report, proposals, or elsewhere, in addition to the items listed under Clause 3.6:

(a) Weighted and unweighted bases for all conventional tables, clearly distinguishing between the two.

(b) A discussion of the effects of the sample design employed, and of any weighting methods used, on the effective size of the sample.

(c) A discussion of any aspects of the research which may bias the results obtained from it.

(d) In the case of desk research, an assessment of the reliability of the sources used.

(e) The name of the executive responsible for the research (where more than one has made a significant contribution the name of each and his responsibilities should be given).
A list of any sampling points used in the research project and an adequate

description of all quality control methods used also to be made available on request.

3.15 Members, when presenting the results of a project (whether such presentation is as written or oral description, or in any other form), to make a clear distinction between the objective results and their own opinions and recommendations.

3.16 The research agency to be informed in advance if the client intends a wider circulation of the results of the study, either in whole or in part, and given an opportunity to express an opinion on:

(a) the exact form and contents of the publication or circulation and

(b) the items under Clauses 3.6 and 3.14 which should be provided to recipients of this wider circulation, on request and at the enquirer's expense if necessary. (See also Clauses 3.11, 5.3 and 5.6.)

PART IV: RESPONSIBILITIES TO OUTSIDE CONTRACTORS

Responsibilities to Outside Contractors and Field Workers (whether or not members of the professional body)

Definitions

In this section the term 'outside contractor' is intended to cover such bodies as 'field force' companies, data processing houses, 'in house' interviewers, freelance (part-time) interviewers, etc. For the sake of convenience the term 'operator' is used.

Rules of conduct

4.1 The operator shall not be asked to undertake any type of interview or any method of respondent selection, or any other form of work, which is elsewhere disallowed by this Code.

4.2 The operator shall be provided with sufficient information and guidance to enable Clause 2.5 to be met. (See also Good Practice Clause 4.4.)

Good practice

It is considered good practice that:

4.3 The terms and conditions on which work is commissioned from the operator should be clearly set out in writing and agreed by both parties before the work starts.

4.4 Every effort should be made to enable the operator to observe the recommendations of Clauses 2.11 and 2.13. (See also Rule of conduct 4.2.)

PART V: RESPONSIBILITIES TO OTHER THIRD PARTIES

Responsibilities to the General Public, the Business Community and other Institutions

Rules of conduct

5.1 Public confidence in market research shall not be abused.

5.2 No activity shall be deliberately or inadvertently misrepresented as being market research. Specifically, the following activities shall in no way be associated, directly or by implication, with market or social research interviewing:

(a) sales approaches for profit or the compilation of lists for canvassing.
(b) attempts to influence opinions *per se.*
(c) industrial espionage.
(d) enquiries about private individuals *per se.* (See also Good Practice Clause 5.5.)

5.3 A member shall not knowingly disseminate conclusions from a given research project or service which are inconsistent with, or not warranted by, the data. He shall also do his best to restrain any such dissemination by another party which arises from research with which he has been connected. This especially applies to public opinion polls and to the use of market research findings in advertising and sales promotion. (See Clauses 3.11 and 3.16.)

5.4 Letters after names tend to be understood as indicating that the user has an academic or professional qualification. The use of letters after an individual's name such as AMIMRA or FMIMRA can be misleading: members should refrain from using them except in such a form and manner as the professional body, from time to time, shall permit. This, does not, however, preclude members, where relevant, from pointing out that they are Full or Associate members of the professional body.

Good practice

5.5 Quite apart from actually misrepresenting other activities as being market research (see Clause 5.2), it is good practice to take every precaution to avoid leaving informants after a legitimate interview with the impression that they have been subjected to misrepresentation. (See also Clause 2.5(a).)

5.6 It is not good practice to make, or to be a party to the making of, claims based on research without offering to provide details of the research methods. (See Clauses 3.11 and 3.16.)

5.7 If members are approached for an interview which is ostensibly market research but which they suspect or find out to be something else, it is good practice for them to obtain the name of the 'interviewer' and the name and address of the organization involved. If their suspicions are confirmed they should complain directly to the 'interviewer' and to the organization for which he is working and also report the facts to the duly appointed committee of the professional body. Members should report to the same committee any other cases of which they become aware of activities being misrepresented as market research, in breach of Clause 5.2.

It is also good practice for members to report to the committee any cases of which they become aware of market research neglecting its proprer responsibilities to informants, as set out in Part II, or of research conclusions being disseminated which are inconsistent with, or not warranted by, the data on which they are based. This clause applies whether or not a member of the professional body is concerned in the activity on which the report is made.

5.8 Although members are in general at liberty to conduct research into the products or services of the client's competitors, or of other organizations or individuals, without their permission, nevertheless it is not good practice to do it in such a way as to affect their reputation adversely.

PART VI: PROFESSIONAL RESPONSIBILITIES

Rules of conduct

6.1 Members in client companies, if they commission market research work from persons or organizations not known to be bound by this Code of Conduct, shall ensure that they are familiar with its contents and agree in writing to abide by it as if they were in fact members. (See above for the special requirements regarding Part II when commissioning overseas research.)

6.2 A member shall not knowingly place a fellow member in a position in which he may unwittingly breach any mandatory part of this Code of Conduct.

6.3 The most senior member within the hierarchy of an organization (or members if two or more are of equal status) who is a member of the professional body shall take all reasonable steps (e.g. by the display or circulation of suitable notices) to ensure that all relevant individuals in that organization are familiar with this Code of Conduct, and that the working arrangements of the organization are such that the Code is unlikely to be breached through ignorance of its provisions. This, of course, does not absolve members of the professional body in the organization of their own individual responsibilities.

Good practice

6.4 It is good practice for senior members in research agencies (see Clause 6.3) which conduct product tests or do other forms of research which involve the possibility of risk to informants, however slight, to ensure that the agency indemnifies itself against claims for compensation by carrying appropriate insurance.

6.5 It is good practice when considering interviews with members of small populations likely to be of interest to researchers to be especially careful to avoid unnecessary interviews, since there is a particular danger that such populations may become 'over-researched'. For the same reason it would be good practice for members interested in such populations to combine to undertake syndicated research rather than each separately commissioning their own projects. (See also Clause 2.14.)

6.6 It is not good practice for a member to take advantage, without permission, of the unpublished work of a fellow member in another organization. Specifically, it is not good practice for a member to carry out or commission a research project based on a proposal prepared by a member in another organization, unless permission has been obtained from that organization.

6.7 When writing to the press, or making any similar communication, members are at liberty to claim membership of the professional body if they so wish. It is not good practice, however, to do this in any way which would imply that they are writing or speaking on behalf of the professional body, unless they have the authority of Council, or some duly delegated individual or committee, to do so.

6.8 Guidance to members aware of an actual or potential breach in the mandatory parts of this Code of Conduct:

Four circumstances can be distinguished:

(a) Where the member is instructed to breach a mandatory part of the Code by his superior in the organization.

In these circumstances the member must not, of course, obey the instruction. He should explain this to his superior, by reference to this Code if necessary, and may ask the duly appointed committee of the professional body to confirm to the superior that the required action would be a breach of the Code. In cases where it is not completely clear whether or not the proposed action would be a breach of the Code, it would be good practice to consult the duly appointed committee, which is prepared to advise members before a decision is taken.

(b) Where the breach is about to occur on a survey with which the member is connected.

If the member is aware of a breach before it has taken place, he should do his best to prevent it, lest he be considered to be a party to the breach. Where the member is not the individual responsible for the survey he should point out, in writing, to the person responsible for the project that the proposed action would be a breach of the Code. (Copies of any written communications should, of course, be retained.) If necessary he should also seek the support of other members of the professional body working for the organization, especially the senior member (see Clause 6.3), and may request advice from the duly appointed committee of the professional body.

(c) If a member only becomes aware of a breach on a project with which he is connected after it has taken place, he should:

(i) Ensure that those responsible for the survey are aware that it is, in fact, a breach, and thus attempt to prevent a recurrence.

(ii) Ensure that all concerned in the organization do their utmost to minimize any damage caused by the breach. If difficulties arise in this respect because the member is not the person responsible for the research, then he should proceed as in the appropriate part of Clause 6.8(b) above. If required, the duly appointed committee of the professional body is prepared to give advice in these circumstances and, in extreme cases, a written report should be sent to the committee.

(d) Where a member has no connection with the project but becomes aware of a breach, he should remind the person responsible for the project, if he is a member, of his responsibilities. If the person responsible for the project is not a member, he should inform the senior member of the professional body (see Clause 6.3) in the organization. Such communications should preferably be in writing. (Copies of any written communications should, of course, be retained.) If the breach continues, the member should proceed as in Clause 6.8(b) or (c)—in particular seeking the support of other members of the professional body in the organization and, if needs be, informing the duly appointed committee of the professional body.

Appendix 2: A Checklist for Marketing Researchers

(a) THE COMPANY'S ENVIRONMENT

1.0 The Company

1. What is the image and reputation of the company?
2. What are the major strengths of the company?
3. What is the current and historical profit record?
4. What is the current and historical cost record?
5. How effective are the marketing functions of the company?
   —Marketing Research Department
   —Distribution methods
   —Selling methods
   —Advertising policies
   —Sales promotion methods

2.0 The Product

1. What are the different company products usef for?
2. What are the major product advantages?
3. What are the major product weaknesses?
4. What is the image of the products?
5. What is the image of the different brands?
6. At what stage in the product life-cycle is the product?
7. How is the product purchased?
8. How frequently is the product purchased?
9. Are there any substitutes for the product?
10. Are there any potential changes or modifications to be made to the product?
11. What product changes have been made over the past five years?
12. Are there any new product developments?
13. What are the potential changes and developments in materials used?
14. How stable is the supply of the product?

3.0 Sales

1. What are the sales of the company?
2. What are the sales by product?
3. What are the sales by market segment?
4. What are the sales by geographical area?
5. What are the sales by distribution outlet?
6. What are the sales by type and size of product?
7. What selling methods are employed?
8. How is the sales force organized?
9. How effective are the services provided to aid the sales force?

4.0 The Customer

1. Who are the customers?
2. What are the characteristics of the customer?
3. What is the customer profile?
4. Where are the customers located?
5. How loyal are the customers
   —to the company?
   —to the products?
   —to the brands?
6. How satisfied are the customers
   —with the product?
   —with the company?
   —with the services of the company?

5.0 The Market

1. What is the size of the total market?
2. How can the market be segmented
   —geographically?
   —by type and size of product?
   —by users?
   —by distribution outlets?
   —by industry?
3. How is the market structured?
4. What are the geographical or seasonal variations?
5. What are the trends in the market?
   —size
   —structure
   —market
6. What are the market opportunities for growth?
7. What are the major limitation factors to growth?
8. What is the market share of the company?
   —in the total market

—by size and type of product
—by geographical region
—by type of user?
9. What percentage of the UK market is accounted for by imported products?
10. What are the major developments in the market?
—current
—past
—future

6.0 Competitors

1. What is the image of the leading competitors?
2. What is the image of the main competitive products?
3. What is the quality image of the main competitors?
4. What are the main product similarities between the company and its major competitors?
5. What are the major product differences between the company and its major competitors?
6. What are the major strengths and weaknesses of the competitors and their products?
7. What are the market shares of the major competitors?
8. What are the principal market segments of the major competitors?
9. How do the services offered by the major competitors differ?
10. How does the sales promotion or advertising policies of major competitors differ?
11. How do the distribution methods of major competitors differ?
12. How do the selling methods of major competitors differ?
13. How do the pricing and discount policies of the major competitors differ?
14. Do competitors give more lenient credit terms?
15. What are the major developments and potential changes in competitors?

7.0 International

1. What are the potential export markets?
2. What are the characteristics of the potential export markets?
—size
—profile
3. How can the potential markets be segmented?
—by geographical area
—by demographic characteristics
—by distributors
—by users
—by industry
—by type of product
4. How will climatic conditions affect the product and its packaging?

5.   What are the distribution methods available?
6.   What would be the cost of selling in foreign markets?
7.   Which major competitors are already established in the potential markets?
8.   Are the products manufactured in the country?
9.   Who are the major producers?
10. Are there any import restrictions or quotas?
11. Are there any current licensing agreements?
12. What are the technical regulations?
13. Are there any protectionist policies?
14. What are the current economic and trading conditions?
15. How politically stable is the country?
16. How will the differences in language and culture affect the marketing of the product?
17. Are there any developments and plans?
18. What special selling methods and aids that will be required?

(b)   THE EXTERNAL ENVIRONMENT

1.0   Technology

1.   What have been the recent technological developments affecting the product?
2.   What is the rate of change in technological factors affecting the product?
3.   How can technological developments influence the development of new products?
4.   What are the potential changes in technology of the company?
5.   How does the technological developments of the company compare to that of competitors?

2.0   Economic Factors

1.   How stable is the present economy?
2.   What are the macro economic developments?
3.   What are the current trends in the economy?
4.   What are the potential changes in economic policy?
5.   Is the economy buoyant, stable or dormant?
6.   What economic restrictions are there?
7.   What are the current economic policies on taxation, credit, prices?
8.   What are the current attitudes in the economic climate?

3.0   Social Factors

1.   What are the attitudes to consumerism in the market sectors of the company?
2.   What are the current attitudes to industry?

3. What changes have there been in the social strata?
4. What changes have there been in social habits in recent years?
5. Has there been any changes in the demographic characteristics of the population in recent years?
6. What are the current social trends?

4.0 Government Policies

1. What are the present attitudes of the government to industry?
2. How stable are the government policies?
3. What is the government attitude to price agreements and restrictive trade practices?
4. What new legislation is to be introduced, e.g. on
   —safety
   —quality control methods
   —consumer protection?
5. What are the current government policies on
   —support of industry
   —subsidies

Appendix 3: Random Number Tables

```
03 47 43 73 86    36 96 47 36 61    46 98 63 71 62    33 26 16 80 45    60 11 14 10 95
97 74 24 67 62    42 81 14 57 20    42 53 32 37 32    27 07 36 07 51    24 51 79 89 73
16 76 62 27 66    56 50 26 71 07    32 90 79 78 53    13 55 38 58 59    88 97 54 14 10
12 56 85 99 26    96 96 68 27 31    05 03 72 93 15    57 12 10 14 21    88 26 49 81 76
55 59 56 35 64    38 54 82 46 22    31 62 43 09 90    06 18 44 32 53    23 83 01 30 30

16 22 77 94 39    49 54 43 54 82    17 37 93 23 78    87 35 20 96 43    84 26 34 91 64
84 42 17 53 31    57 24 55 06 88    77 04 74 47 67    21 76 33 50 25    83 92 12 06 76
63 01 63 78 59    16 95 55 67 19    98 10 50 71 75    12 86 73 58 07    44 39 52 38 79
33 21 12 34 29    78 64 56 07 82    52 42 07 44 38    15 51 00 13 42    99 66 02 79 54
57 60 86 32 44    09 47 27 96 54    49 17 46 09 62    90 52 84 77 27    08 02 73 43 28

18 18 07 92 46    44 17 16 58 09    79 83 86 19 62    06 76 50 03 10    55 23 64 05 05
26 62 38 97 75    84 16 07 44 99    83 11 46 32 24    20 14 85 88 45    10 93 72 88 71
23 42 40 64 74    82 97 77 77 81    07 45 32 14 08    32 98 94 07 72    93 85 79 10 75
52 36 28 19 95    50 92 26 11 97    00 56 76 31 38    80 22 02 53 53    86 60 42 04 53
37 85 94 35 12    83 39 50 08 30    42 34 07 96 88    54 42 06 87 98    35 85 29 48 39

70 29 17 12 13    40 33 20 38 26    13 89 51 03 74    17 76 37 13 04    07 74 21 19 30
56 62 18 37 35    96 83 50 87 75    97 12 25 93 47    70 33 24 03 54    97 77 46 44 80
99 49 57 22 77    88 42 95 45 72    16 64 36 16 00    04 43 18 66 79    94 77 24 21 90
16 08 15 04 72    33 27 14 34 09    45 59 34 68 49    12 72 07 34 45    99 27 72 95 14
31 16 93 32 43    50 27 89 87 19    20 15 37 00 49    52 85 66 60 44    38 68 88 11 80

68 34 30 13 70    55 74 30 77 40    44 22 78 84 26    04 33 46 09 52    68 07 97 06 57
74 57 25 65 76    59 29 97 68 60    71 91 38 67 54    13 58 18 24 76    15 54 55 95 52
27 42 37 86 53    48 55 90 65 72    96 57 69 36 10    96 46 92 42 45    97 60 49 04 91
00 39 68 29 61    66 37 32 20 30    77 84 57 03 29    10 45 65 04 26    11 04 96 67 24
29 94 98 94 24    68 49 69 10 82    53 75 91 93 30    34 25 20 57 27    40 48 73 51 92

16 90 82 66 59    83 62 64 11 12    67 19 00 71 74    60 47 21 29 68    02 02 37 03 31
11 27 94 75 06    06 09 19 74 66    02 94 37 34 02    76 70 90 30 86    38 45 94 30 38
35 24 10 16 20    33 32 51 26 38    79 78 45 04 91    16 92 53 56 16    02 75 50 95 98
38 23 16 86 38    42 38 97 01 50    87 75 66 81 41    40 01 74 91 62    48 51 84 08 32
31 96 25 91 47    96 44 33 49 13    34 86 82 53 91    00 52 43 48 85    27 55 26 89|62

66 67 40 67 14    64 05 71 95 86    11 05 65 09 68    76 83 20 37 90    57 16 00 11 66
14 90 84 45 11    75 73 88 05 90    52 27 41 14 86    22 98 12 22 08    07 52 74 95 80
68 05 51 18 00    33 96 02 75 19    07 60 62 93 55    59 33 82 43 90    49 37 38 44 59
20 46 78 73 90    97 51 40 14 02    04 02 33 31 08    39 54 16 49 36    47 95 93 13 30
64 19 58 97 79    15 06 15 93 20    01 90 10 75 06    40 78 78 89 62    02 67 74 17 33

05 26 93 70 60    22 35 85 15 13    92 03 51 59 77    59 56 78 06 83    52 91 05 70 74
07 97 10 88 23    09 98 42 99 64    61 71 62 99 15    06 51 29 16 93    58 05 77 09 51
68 71 86 85 85    54 87 66 47 54    73 32 08 11 12    44 95 92 63 16    29 56 24 29 48
26 99 61 65 53    58 37 78 80 70    42 10 50 67 42    32 17 55 85 74    94 44 67 16 94
14 65 52 68 75    87 59 36 22 41    26 78 63 06 55    13 08 27 01 50    15 29 39 39 43

17 53 77 58 71    71 41 61 50 72    12 41 94 96 26    44 95 27 36 99    02 96 74 30 83
90 26 59 21 19    23 52 23 33 12    96 93 02 18 39    07 02 18 36 07    25 99 32 70 23
41 23 52 55 99    31 04 49 69 96    10 47 48 45 88    13 41 43 89 20    97 17 14 49 17
60 20 50 81 69    31 99 73 68 68    35 81 33 03 76    24 30 12 48 60    18 99 10 72 34
91 25 38 05 90    94 58 28 41 36    45 37 59 03 09    90 35 57 29 12    82 62 54 65 60

34 50 57 74 37    98 80 33 00 91    09 77 93 19 82    74 94 80 04 04    45 07 31 66 49
85 22 04 39 43    73 81 53 94 79    33 62 46 86 28    08 31 54 46 31    53 94 13 38 47
09 79 13 77 48    73 82 97 22 21    05 03 27 24 83    72 89 44 05 60    35 80 39 94 88
88 75 80 18 14    22 95 75 42 49    39 32 82 22 49    02 48 07 70 37    16 04 61 67 87
90 96 23 70 00    39 00 03 06 90    55 85 78 38 36    94 37 30 69 32    90 89 00 76 33
```

106

107

(Reproduced from J. Murdoch and J. A. Bornes, *Statistical Tables*, by permission of Macmillan, London and Basingstoke)

53 74 23 99 67	61 32 28 69 84	94 62 67 86 24	98 33 41 19 95	47 53 38 53 09
63 38 06 86 54	99 00 65 26 94	02 82 90 23 07	79 62 67 80 60	75 91 12 81 19
35 30 58 21 46	06 72 17 10 94	25 21 31 75 96	49 28 24 00 49	55 65 79 78 07
63 43 36 82 69	65 51 18 37 88	61 38 44 12 45	32 92 85 88 65	54 34 81 85 35
98 25 37 55 26	01 91 82 81 46	74 71 12 94 97	24 02 71 37 07	03 92 18 66 75
02 63 21 17 69	71 50 80 89 56	38 15 70 11 48	43 40 45 86 98	00 83 26 91 03
64 55 22 21 82	48 22 28 06 00	61 54 13 43 91	82 78 12 23 29	06 66 24 12 27
85 07 26 13 89	01 10 07 82 04	59 63 69 36 03	69 11 15 83 80	13 29 54 19 28
58 54 16 24 15	51 54 44 82 00	62 61 65 04 69	38 18 65 18 97	85 72 13 49 21
34 85 27 84 87	61 48 64 56 26	90 18 48 13 26	37 70 15 42 57	65 65 30 39 07
03 92 18 27 46	57 99 16 96 56	30 33 72 85 22	84 64 38 56 98	99 01 30 98 64
62 95 30 27 59	37 75 41 66 48	86 97 80 61 45	23 53 04 01 63	45 76 08 64 27
08 45 93 15 22	60 21 75 46 91	98 77 27 85 42	28 88 61 08 84	69 62 03 42 73
07 08 55 18 40	45 44 75 13 90	24 94 96 61 02	57 55 66 83 15	73 42 37 11 61
01 85 89 95 66	51 10 19 34 88	15 84 97 19 75	12 76 39 43 78	64 63 91 08 25
72 84 71 14 35	19 11 58 49 26	50 11 17 17 76	86 31 57 20 18	95 60 78 46 75
88 78 28 16 84	13 52 53 94 53	75 45 69 30 96	73 89 65 70 31	99 17 43 48 76
45 17 75 65 57	28 40 19 72 12	25 12 74 75 67	60 40 60 81 19	24 62 01 61 16
96 76 28 12 54	22 01 11 94 25	71 96 16 16 88	68 64 36 74 45	19 59 50 88 92
43 31 67 72 30	24 02 94 08 63	38 32 36 66 02	69 36 38 25 39	48 03 45 15 22
50 44 66 44 21	66 06 58 05 62	68 15 54 35 02	42 35 48 96 32	14 52 41 52 48
22 66 22 15 86	26 63 75 41 99	58 42 36 72 24	58 37 52 18 51	03 37 18 39 11
96 24 40 14 51	23 22 30 88 57	95 67 47 29 83	94 69 40 06 07	18 16 36 78 86
31 73 91 61 19	60 20 72 93 48	98 57 07 23 69	65 95 39 69 58	56 80 30 19 44
78 60 73 99 84	43 89 94 36 45	56 69 47 07 41	90 22 91 07 12	78 35 34 08 72
84 37 90 61 56	70 10 23 98 05	85 11 34 76 60	76 48 45 34 60	01 64 18 39 96
36 67 10 08 23	98 93 35 08 86	99 29 76 29 81	33 34 91 58 93	63 14 52 32 52
07 28 59 07 48	89 64 58 89 75	83 85 62 27 89	30 14 78 56 27	86 63 59 80 02
10 15 83 87 60	79 24 31 66 56	21 48 24 06 93	91 98 94 05 49	01 47 59 38 00
55 19 68 97 65	03 73 52 16 56	00 53 55 90 27	33 42 29 38 87	22 13 88 83 34
53 81 29 13 39	35 01 20 71 34	62 33 74 82 14	53 73 19 09 03	56 54 29 56 93
51 86 32 68 92	33 98 74 66 99	40 14 71 94 58	45 94 19 38 81	14 44 99 81 07
35 91 70 29 13	80 03 54 07 27	96 94 78 32 66	50 95 52 74 33	13 80 55 62 54
37 71 67 95 13	20 02 44 95 94	64 85 04 05 72	01 32 90 76 14	53 89 74 60 41
93 66 13 83 27	92 79 64 64 72	28 54 96 53 84	48 14 52 98 94	56 07 93 89 30
02 96 08 45 65	13 05 00 41 84	93 07 54 72 59	21 45 57 09 77	19 48 56 27 44
49 83 43 48 35	82 88 33 69 96	72 36 04 19 76	47 45 15 18 60	82 11 08 95 97
84 60 71 62 46	40 80 81 30 37	34 39 23 05 38	25 15 35 71 30	88 12 57 21 77
18 17 30 88 71	44 91 14 88 47	89 23 30 63 15	56 34 20 47 89	99 82 93 24 98
79 69 10 61 78	71 32 76 95 62	87 00 22 58 40	92 54 01 75 25	43 11 71 99 31
75 93 36 57 83	56 20 14 82 11	74 21 97 90 65	96 42 68 63 86	74 54 13 26 94
38 30 92 29 03	06 28 81 39 38	62 25 06 84 63	61 29 08 93 67	04 32 92 08 09
51 29 50 10 34	31 57 75 95 80	51 97 02 74 77	76 15 48 49 44	18 55 63 77 09
21 31 38 86 24	37 79 81 53 74	73 24 16 10 33	52 83 90 94 76	70 47 14 54 36
29 01 23 87 88	58 02 39 37 67	42 10 14 20 92	16 55 23 42 45	54 96 09 11 06
95 33 95 22 00	18 74 72 00 18	38 79 58 69 32	81 76 80 26 92	82 80 84 25 39
90 84 60 79 80	24 36 59 87 38	82 07 53 89 35	96 35 23 79 18	05 98 90 07 35
46 40 62 93 82	54 97 20 56 95	15 74 80 08 32	16 46 70 50 80	67 72 16 42 79
20 31 89 03 43	38 46 82 68 72	32 14 82 99 70	80 60 47 18 97	63 49 30 21 30
71 59 73 05 50	08 22 23 71 77	91 01 93 20 49	82 96 59 26 94	66 39 67 98 60

References

1. Rawnsley, A. (Ed.), *Manual of Industrial Marketing Research*, John Wiley, 1978, Chapter 2.
2. Crosier, K., 'What exactly is Marketing?' *Quarterly Review of Marketing* Winter 1975, 21–5.
3. McCarthy, E. S., *Basic Marketing, A Managerial Approach*, Revised edn, Richard D. Irwin, pp. 38–44.
4. CBD Research Publications, *Directory of British Associations*, CBD Research Publications, 1979.
5. Delens, A. H. R., *Principles of Market Research*, Crosby Lockwood, 1964.
6. Finsterbush, K., *Methodology of Social Impact Assessment*, Dowden, Hutchinson and Ross, 1978.
7. Wilson, A., *The Assessment of Industrial Markets*, Associated Business Programmes, 1973, Chapter 8, pp. 192–3.
8. De Bono, E., *Po, Beyond Yes and No*, Penguin, 1972.
9. Likert, R., 'The Method of Constructing an Attitude Scale' in *Readings in Attitude Theory and Measurements*, John Wiley, 1932.
10. Osgood C. E., Suci, G. J., and Tannerbaum, P. M., *The Measurement of Meaning*, University of Illinois Press, 1957.
11. Hughes G. D., 'Upgrading the Semantic Differential', *Journal of the Marketing Research Society*, **17**, 41–4.
12. Evans, R. H., 'The Upgraded Semantic Differential: A Further Test', *Journal of the Marketing Research Society*, **22**, No. 2, 143–7.

Select Bibliography

Boyd, Westfall and Stasch, *Marketing Research: Text and Cases*, 4th edn, Richard D. Irwin, 1977.
Cateora, P. R., and Mess, J. M., *International Marketing*, Richard D. Irwin, 1975.
Chisnall, P. M., *Effective Industrial Marketing*, Longman, 1977.
Crosier, K., 'What Exactly is Marketing?' *Quarterly Review of Marketing* Winter 1975, 21–5.
De Bono, E., *Po, Beyond Yes and No*, Penguin, 1972.
Delens, A. H. R., *Principles of Market Research*, Crosby Lockwood, 1964.
Evans, R. H., 'The Upgraded Semantic Differential: A Further Test', *Journal of Marketing Research Society*, **22**, No. 2.
Finsterbush, K., *Methodology of Social Impact Assessment*, Dowden, Hutchinson and Ross, 1978.
Hughes, D. G., 'Upgrading the Semantic Differential', *Journal of the Marketing Society*, **17**.
ISBA, *Research Reports*, The Incorporated Society of British Advertisers Ltd.
Kotler, P., *Marketing Management: Analysis, Planning and Control*, 4th edn, Prentice-Hall, 1980.
Likert, R., 'The Method of Constructing an Attitude Scale', *Readings in Attitude Theory and Measurement*, John Wiley, 1932.
McCarthy, E. S., *Basic Marketing, A Managerial Approach*, Revised edn, Richard D. Irwin, 1964.
Mirror Group Newspapers, *MGN Marketing Manual*, Mirror Group Newspapers Limited, annual.
Osgood, C. E., Suci, G. J., and Tannerbaum, P. M., *The Measurement of Meaning*, University of Illinois Press, 1957.
Rawnsley, A., *Manual of Industrial Marketing Research*, John Wiley, 1978.
Schaffin, K. H., and Trentin, M. G., *Marketing Information Systems*, Amacon, 1973.
Thomas, M. J. 'International Marketing Management' in *Readings in Systems and Method*, Houghton Mifflin, 1969.
Thorelli, H. B. (Ed.), *International Marketing Strategy*, Penguin, 1973.
Tull, D. S., and Hawkins, D. I., 'Marketing Research' in *Meaning, Measurement and Method*, Macmillan Publishing Co., 1976.
Tupper E. and Wills, G., *Sources of UK Marketing Information*, (Marketing Research Society), Ernest Benn.
Wilmhurst, J., *The Fundamentals and Practice of Marketing*, Heinemann, 1979.
Wilson, A., *The Assessment of Industrial Markets*, Associated Business Programmes, 1973.

Index